Does It Matter
What I Believe?

Does It Matter What I Believe?

What the Bible Teaches and Why We Should Believe It

Millard J. Erickson

**Study Guides and
Teaching Suggestions
by Sandra McMaken**

BAKER BOOK HOUSE
Grand Rapids, Michigan 49516

Library of Congress Cataloging-in-Publication Data

Erickson, Millard J.

 Does it matter what I believe? / Millard J. Erickson;
study guides and teaching suggestions by Sandra
McMaken.
  p. cm.
 ISBN 0-8010-3214-8
 1. Theology—Biblical. 2. Sermons, American. I.
McMaken, Sandra. II. Title.
 BX6333.E75D64 1992
 252'.061—dc20
             92-5644

To three thoughtful groups of Christians
who reflected together with me on the matters
in these pages

Cross of Glory Baptist Church
Hopkins, Minnesota

Calvary Baptist Church
St. Cloud, Minnesota

Brooklyn Center Baptist Church
Brooklyn Center, Minnesota

Contents

Preface

In the twenty-seven years since I left the full-time pastorate to enter teaching, I have sought to utilize the local church as a laboratory. The forty-one interim preaching pastorates that I have been privileged to serve during that period (some of the congregations two and even three times) have provided me with continuing education in ministry, teaching me even as I sought to teach. Explaining on a popular level the doctrines that I teach in a seminary classroom, I have found a strong and persistent theological interest among many laypersons. Frequently the questions laypersons ask equal the quality of the questions which theological students pose.

It is with such persons in mind that this small volume was written. It reflects a series of Sunday evening messages which I have presented in several congregations. The final form was drafted in connection with a series of Sunday evening studies at the Brooklyn Center Baptist Church, Brooklyn Center, Minnesota. It is my hope that this book will serve to introduce many lay Christians to a systematic presentation of doctrine, building them up in the faith and even leading some to a more advanced study. Suggestions for additional reading will be found at the end of each chapter. Persons wishing to go more deeply into the study of these matters are also referred to two other volumes I have written: *Christian Theology* (Baker, 1986), and *Introducing Christian Doctrine* (Baker, 1992).

The present book has been written not only for lay Christians who wish to deepen their understanding, however. I also have sought to design it for persons who are inquiring as to what Christianity is about or who are confused in their beliefs. In our day of many competing religions and secular belief systems, it is increasingly important to be clear regarding the basic doctrines of Christianity.

I appreciate greatly the work done by Sandra McMaken in preparing study questions and suggestions for the teacher. These helpful materials substantially increase the usefulness of the book. Her knowledge both of theology and of Christian education, combined with her current adult ministry in a suburban Minneapolis congregation, is reflected in her eminently appropriate and practical contributions. Once again, Ray Wiersma of Baker Book House has greatly enhanced the final product, and Allan Fisher of Baker has offered very helpful general comments.

This book is sent forth with the prayer that it will help to provide what the writer of the Letter to the Hebrews desired for his readers: "solid food . . . for the mature, who by constant use have trained themselves to distinguish good from evil" (Heb. 5:14 NIV).

1

Does It Matter What I Believe?

"Does it matter what I believe?" the young woman asked me. "If I love Jesus, isn't that enough? Do I have to believe all those things about creation and sin and being born again, too? And do I have to believe that people who don't believe those things are going to hell?" She was neither the first nor the last person to raise questions like that. To some, even Christians, doctrinal beliefs seem more of a hindrance than a help. Requiring belief in specific teachings seems to be keeping some people out of the church and even to be keeping Christians apart. In an age in which there is so much emphasis, even within the church, upon understanding and feeling good about oneself and one's relationships with others, how important are our beliefs about such matters as sin and the Holy Spirit?

The Necessity of Having Correct Beliefs

In answering such questions, we as Christians naturally turn first to what Christ himself had to say on the subject. What people believed about him was very important to Jesus. After asking what people believed about him and hearing the disciples' recital of the various opinions which were current at the time, he then asked the disciples who they said that he was. Only when Peter, speaking on behalf of the disciples, declared that Jesus was the Christ, the Son of the living God, did Jesus pronounce him blessed and entrust the authority of the kingdom of heaven to the disciples (Matt. 16:13–19). One of the disciples in that group was John, who later wrote of the importance of believing both in the deity and in the humanity of Jesus (1 John 4:2–3; 5:5–10). Moreover, Paul indicated in Romans 10:9–10 that to be saved one must believe in the resurrection of Jesus. And the writer of the Letter to the Hebrews stated that anyone who comes to God must believe in his existence and in his faithfulness in rewarding those who diligently seek him (11:6).

These, however, are beliefs related directly to the one in whom we place our faith. What about the other matters? If correct belief about Jesus is necessary to a proper relationship with him, what about belief regarding some of these other matters, such as sin and baptism? Are they important also? James Orr, a prominent British theologian a century ago, correctly pointed out that when we say with our whole heart that Jesus is Lord, we have thereby accepted much more besides, for we have committed ourselves to Jesus' teaching about God, the human race, sin, redemption, and the various other topics he discussed. If Jesus is Lord, he is Lord of our beliefs as well as of the other areas of our lives. Just as we cannot call him "Lord, Lord," and not do what he says (Luke 6:46), so we cannot call him "Lord, Lord," and not believe the things he teaches. And of course in loving Jesus we will want to know all about him, including what he has done and is doing, and everything he taught.

There are many other reasons why having correct beliefs is important. Our whole lives are inevitably affected by the real world around us, so what we believe about it is of the utmost significance. Some persons have not wanted to hear what the Bible has to say about sin, because it gives them an unpleasant feeling of lack of worthiness. So they avoid thinking about it. They engage instead in "positive thinking." They are like some people who do not go to see their doctor, because they are afraid they may have a serious illness. Unfortunately, their refusal to face reality and act in light of it does not change the condition, except that without any treatment it will probably worsen with the passing of time, and an even more unpleasant situation will occur. What we believe about reality does not change the truth, nor its effect upon us. Correct belief, however, enables us to know the truth as it is, and then to take appropriate action, so that it will have the best possible effect upon our lives.

Having correct beliefs is also necessary because of the large amount and variety of incorrect beliefs which are about. I am not referring here to gross denials or rejections of the central tenets of the Christian faith, such as atheism or communism; rather, I am referring to views which may have a large amount in common with Christianity. They are similar enough to sound attractive, yet different enough to be dangerous.

This is a greater problem today than at most times in the past. For one thing, we are being assaulted by other world religions, even in the United States. There was a time when we were rather exclusively exporters of religion, as well as of manufactured items. Today, however, that has changed. It is not simply Toyota automobiles and Sony television sets that are being imported from the Far East. There has been a rising influence of Eastern religions, especially with the coming of large numbers of Asians to the West. Some of the ideas found in those religions are beginning to creep into our broader culture and are even being incorporated into the beliefs of some Christians. Some of these ideas sound very much like traditional Christian teachings. They seem to be fresh ways of putting old beliefs. It is important that Christians know what the Bible really teaches, so that we can recognize error.

This is a crucial point. Sometimes we think the way to prevent people from falling into error is to teach them a great deal about all the possible untruths and half-truths they may encounter, so they will recognize error when they see it. Unfortunately, however, this requires exposing people to a large number of erroneous views, some of which would otherwise never enter their minds. In addition to being both very time-consuming and largely unnecessary, it also concentrates much of one's attention upon the negative. This can have an unfortunate effect, like a golfer's concentrating on how she is not going to hit the ball, or a cook's emphasizing how he is not going to prepare a particular dish. While we need to be aware of false teaching and what is wrong with it, we are probably better advised to make sure that we really know the truth. Then we will be able to recognize error by its contrast with the truth. This is the procedure which federal governments and banks follow in training persons to recognize counterfeit money. Trainees are not exposed to countless counterfeit bills, but examine genuine bills both visually and tactilely; those features of the genuine currency which are especially difficult to duplicate are painstakingly pointed out. Then, when presented with a bogus bill, new recruits immediately recognize it as such, for they know what they are measuring it against.

Objections to the Study of Doctrine

Are there not some dangers in an extensive concern with the doctrines of our Christian belief? Some Christians are leery of theology, and with some justifiable cause. They can recite horror stories of unfortunate incidents related to theology, which is simply an organized study of the doctrines of the Christian faith. Let us take a few moments to examine some of these objections to the study of Christian doctrine.

1. *The study of doctrine unduly complicates the Christian faith.* It takes that which is simple and makes it complex, thus robbing the Christian experience of its joy and freshness and spontaneity. Having to think about the Christian life robs it of its vitality.

Of course, like anything else, too self-conscious a treatment of the Christian life can distort it. Too much analysis can lead to its drying up. Dissection of a living organism destroys it, and some lovers have done so much analyzing of their relationship that it fades and withers. Or consider the story of the centipede that was able to walk without difficulty until one day someone asked him, "How do you do that? It must be very difficult to coordinate the movements of so many legs." As he began to think about how he moved all of his legs, he was overwhelmed by the complexity of the endeavor and soon found himself unable to walk.

Overanalysis is a proper concern. But the problem does not stem from theology, but from its abuse. Knowing what makes something work is not a disadvantage, but an advantage. The difficulty comes when we are concerned about theory under the wrong circumstances. Suppose that every time a clarinetist played a note, she had to think as follows: "I am going to play a higher note, which means that the frequency of sound waves must be greater, which in turn requires a shorter wavelength, which is produced by a shorter column of vibrating air, so I should push this particular valve on my clarinet." Under such conditions, she probably would not play very well.

Similarly, when I start my car, I don't have to go through a lengthy analysis: "When I turn the key, the starter switch closes, causing electrical current to flow to the starter motor, which causes the crankshaft of the engine to turn. That causes the pistons to rise and fall in their cylinders. It also turns the camshaft, causing the intake and exhaust valves in each cylinder to open and close. As the piston moves downward, it draws a mixture of air and gasoline from the carburetor into the cylinder through the open intake valve. Then, when the piston reaches the bottom of the cylinder, the intake valve closes, so that as the piston moves upward, the fuel-and-air mixture is compressed. Then at just the right moment the distributor, which also is being rotated by this mechanical process, sends a spark of electricity developed by the ignition coil from the battery to the spark plug located in the combustion chamber of the cylinder. A spark leaps between the two electrodes of the spark plug, causing the gasoline mixture to explode, which forces the piston downward, turning the crankshaft and enabling this process to continue without any further work by the starter motor. All of this means that the wheels which are connected to the engine through the drive train (transmission, etc.) will turn, thus causing the car to move."

That all sounds complicated, doesn't it, even in this simplified version? It is a good thing I don't have to think about all of that to start my car. Ordinarily, there is no need to know about this process. All one has to know is where to insert the key, how to turn it, how to put the car in gear, and how to steer it. It is also helpful, of course, to know such things as how to operate the brakes and turn off the ignition. But on those unfortunate occasions when my car does not start, it may be helpful to know something of the theory that I have elaborated above. It is especially important, of course, that mechanics know these things, and so they study such matters at greater length. But it is also helpful to the car owner to know enough to make some minor repairs or do the right things to make the car start. Doctors, of course, must study a great deal about the human body and how it works. All of us, however, will be better able to take care of ourselves if we possess some knowledge of the basic principles of health. In a similar fashion, pastors study theology in considerable depth, but laypersons also need to have some knowledge of it. It is an advantage, not a disadvantage, to know and understand our faith, though there are times when we need to practice it, not think about it.

2. *Doctrine divides Christians.* A common complaint is that doctrine is the reason for the existence of so many different churches. People who are Christians should all work together; their organizations ought not compete with one another. This of course is a serious matter, for Jesus prayed that his followers might be one, as he and the Father are one (John 17:21). Is doctrine the culprit in frustrating this concern of Jesus?

Actually, there are many reasons why Christians are part of different congregations. One is simple geography. Christians who live at a considerable distance from one another are members of different congregations not out of anger with one another, but simply because of practical considerations of location. Or churches may be separate because they have somewhat different emphases, one concentrating on worship and another on Christian education. The different emphases may reflect the dominant socioeconomic group in the respective communities, one relating more to business executives, and another geared to reaching blue-collar workers. And ethnic groups may carry on their worship in their own languages, one worshiping in Spanish, for example, and another in Vietnamese. They may differ in the way they carry on their ministry, one church emphasizing friendship evangelism while another stresses confrontational evangelism. Or there may be genuine differences in some of the doctrines held.

To be sure, unity is an important quality among Christians. With this goal in view, we need to do two things. First, we need to evaluate the degree of importance of various doctrines. This is not to say that some doctrines are not important, but that some are more crucial than others. In general, the central doctrines are more clearly taught in the Bible than are the less important ones. It is more important to believe that God created everything that is than to agree on how much time he took to create. It is more important to agree that the Lord is going to return in the future, personally, bodily, and visibly, than to agree on the exact time when he will come. Second, we need to think through the degree of doctrinal agreement that is needed for specific kinds of unity. A greater amount of agreement on doctrine is necessary for two people to be part of the same congregation, engaged in ongoing full-orbed ministry, than is needed to cooperate in a citywide evangelistic campaign. The problem comes when people who should be able to work together are separated because they feel they must agree upon some very minute point of doctrine.

3. *Doctrine may distract us from other aspects of the Christian life.* It is possible to become so enamored of doctrine in and of itself that one never gets around to evangelism or worship. This phenomenon occurs in other areas as well; for example, a business executive may become so entranced by his computer that he spends his time experimenting on it, learning it for its own sake, rather than utilizing it for the purpose for which it was provided. This is a particularly insidious practice, since it may be difficult to distinguish this puttering around from actual working on the computer. In like manner, Christians may be merely students of doctrine who fail to apply it meaningfully. But the problem here is not with the doctrine, but with the failure to maintain a balance in one's Christian life. We can never have too much of a good thing, unless it is pursued at the expense of other good things.

The Starting Point

Where do we begin? One question that we need to address before going on to look at the various areas of Christian doctrine is our starting point. Do we begin with the Bible, in which case we are talking about it as the Word of God even though we have not yet established that there is a God? Or do we start with God, in which case we have not yet established that the Bible is indeed a communication from him?

One approach is to establish the existence of God and something about his nature on some basis other than the Bible; for example, the world around us may be cited as proof of his existence. Then we can go on to see what he has told us in the Bible, his Word. Probably all Christians have been exposed to this approach, which theologians call natural theology. Here the so-called watchmaker argument is frequently utilized. No one who found a watch lying on the ground would assume that the molecules which make it up had just come together by chance to form such a complex device. Clearly, someone purposefully designed it. Similarly, a rational person would not assume that this earth, with all of its complexity and features so well adapted to sustain and facilitate life, just came to be through chance.

There are certain problems with this approach, however. Even if one succeeds in proving from the examination of nature that there is a Supreme Being, is this necessarily the Christian God? There simply is not enough detail in this sort of study to establish that what we have proved is the Christian God rather than that of Judaism, for example, unless we read into nature that which we already know from the Bible; but then we have moved out of the realm of natural or rational theology. We certainly cannot prove the existence of a Triune God, for example, from a rational scrutiny of nature. Further, that God is good can be inferred from nature only if we are very selective in our choice of data. If we take into account the evil in the world—natural catastrophes like earthquakes and tornadoes as well as diseases like cancer—we may wonder whether we have not proved the existence of the devil rather than God. The universe seems to present us with a puzzle.

I believe there is a better way to proceed. Suppose we

consider the Bible and the picture it gives us of God and the world as a purported answer to the puzzle. In many such cases we cannot figure out the answer simply from the puzzle itself; but if an answer is suggested, we may be able to test whether that answer is indeed correct. Without the use of calculating or computing devices, it may be very difficult or impossible to determine what is the eighteenth root of a number. If someone supplies us with the answer, however, we can fairly easily verify that it is correct. Similarly, a combination lock may have sixty-four thousand possible sequences. To come up with the correct combination by trying all of them, one after another, could, at thirty seconds per try and forty hours per week, take as long as three months. But if we are given a particular combination, we can tell within thirty seconds whether it is correct.

Let us then begin with this assumption: There exists a God who has revealed himself to humans, and this knowledge has been preserved for us in the Bible. While it will not be the task of this book to test that hypothesis, we can, through the endeavor known as apologetics, show that this hypothesis fits the historical, scientific, philosophical, and experiential data of life and the world better than does any other scheme. We will begin by examining the Bible, this claimed revelation of God, to see what it is like; and then we will use it to learn more about the God who has revealed himself through it.

Study Guide

Key Questions

1. How would you respond to the questions posed by the young woman at the outset of this chapter— "Does it matter what I believe? If I love Jesus, isn't that enough?"
2. What objections to the study of doctrine have been raised by Christians who are leery of theology? How would you respond to these objections?
3. When formulating Christian doctrine, we need a starting point. Where should we begin—with the Bible or with God? Why?

Bible Investigation

Consider the statements, "Ignorance is bliss" and "What you don't know can't hurt you." Do these statements apply to what believers do not bother to learn about God? In other words, will God hold us accountable for what we are not motivated to learn about him? In order to answer this question, read the account of Jesus' appearance to the disciples on the road to Emmaus in Luke 24:13–27. What was Jesus' attitude toward their lack of knowledge concerning the significance of his life? Do you think God will expect any less of us?

Personal Application

The author states that unity is an important quality among Christians, and that we need to decide what level of doctrinal agreement is needed for specific kinds of unity. He suggests that different levels of agreement are acceptable for different kinds of cooperative efforts. How does this idea challenge your view of ecumenism? To what extent can and should churches of various denominations join forces?

For Further Thought

Evidence of the existence of a god can be deduced from nature, but knowledge of the God who has revealed himself to humans cannot be ascertained apart from Scripture. Do you agree or disagree? Why? See 1 John 2.

Suggested Additional Readings

Lewis, C. S. *Mere Christianity.* New York: Macmillan, 1986.

Lewis, Gordon R. *Decide for Yourself.* Downers Grove, Ill.: Inter-Varsity, 1970.

Little, Paul E. *Know Why You Believe.* Downers Grove, Ill.: Inter-Varsity, 1968.

Muck, Terry C. *Alien Gods on American Turf.* Wheaton, Ill.: Victor, 1990.

Neff, David, ed. *Tough Questions Christians Ask.* Wheaton, Ill.: Victor, 1989.

2

When All Else Fails,
Read the Instruction Book

Bill was proud of his new automobile. He could hardly wait to drive it. He listened somewhat impatiently as the salesman explained to him the various controls. He had asked that it be delivered with a full tank of gas, so he proceeded immediately to enjoy driving it. He drove one hundred, two hundred, three hundred miles without needing to fill the gasoline tank. The needle on the gas gauge fell so slowly from full to empty that he knew he must be getting very good mileage. Finally, at about three hundred miles, he pulled into a self-service gasoline station to fill the tank. But he found he could not open the door to the tank. Evidently, somewhere within the car there was a device that released the latch. He looked over the instrument panel and felt along the side of the front seat, but to no avail. Finally, embarrassed, he went to the attendant and asked, "Do you know how to open the door to the gas tank on a new Mercury Topaz?" "Try inside the glove compartment," was the reply. Bill looked and there it was, a little button which released the latch. And there in the glove compartment was also the owner's manual, which explained where the button was. Bill had not followed the old rule, "When all else fails, read the instruction book."

Many people proceed to use their purchases, even automobiles, without reading the instructions. Sometimes the results are disastrous. Saddest of all are the stories of people who attempt to live life without reading the instruction book. For life is much too complicated to figure out without help, but fortunately the designer of life has given us an instruction book. It is called the Bible.

The Ways in Which God Reveals Himself

How to know God has always been a problem for human beings. The ancient Athenians built altars to their many gods, and then, fearing that they had missed one, built yet another altar to "The Unknown God." The large number of religious organizations listed in the yellow pages indicates the varied methods of searching for God. It would seem as if the quest for God has been largely unsuccessful. Yet this still is life's biggest and most important question: "If there is a God, what does he expect and require of me?"

Actually, God has revealed himself in ways that are available to all human beings at all times. The orderliness of nature (Ps. 19:1–4; Rom. 1:19–20), our internal moral consciousness (Rom. 2:14–16), and the hand of God in history (Ps. 33:8–19) are evidences which anyone may observe. They are sufficient to give us a basis for correctly responding to God, and thus they make us responsible before him (Rom. 1:20). In practice, however, very few if any correctly understand and respond (Rom. 1:21–23). So God has made himself known in ways clearer and more complete than what these general sources provide.

There are several special ways or channels through which God has revealed himself. The first is through actually speaking to the human race. Many of the prophets gave testimony like, "The word of the LORD came to me, saying . . ." (Jer. 18:1; Ezek. 12:1; Hos. 1:1; Joel 1:1; Amos 3:1). Sometimes God's messages came through dreams, as in the case of Nebuchadnezzar (Dan. 4:1–18). At other times God spoke through visions: individuals who were fully conscious nonetheless perceived that God was speaking to them, as when Isaiah saw the Lord high and lifted up (Isa. 6). At still other times there was no audible voice, but the Spirit of God was at work in a writer: the very thoughts that came to mind were made known by God.

A second form of God's communication to the human race is through direct action. God has intervened in history; certain events are clear demonstrations of his nature. The Passover, for example, was a demonstration of both God's power and righteousness. The sending of fire at Mount Carmel is another example. Here we have not merely a description but a demonstration of the truth about him.

A third mode of God's making himself known combines the first two and adds yet another important feature. It is one thing to say something about oneself, to send a message. It is something else to act in history, to produce effects which can be observed. But more than that, God actually came into human history; he became a human being without ceasing to be God. This revelation by incarnation is his fullest self-disclosure. Accordingly, John could say that in Jesus he and the other disciples had direct experience of God: "That which was from the beginning, which we have heard, which we have seen with our eyes, which we have looked upon and touched with our hands" (1 John 1:1). This was an amazing statement, especially to the Greeks, for whom touch was the most basic sense. To have actually laid hands upon God was an amazing claim, and an amazing concept. Those who saw Jesus saw the love of God being lived by God in their own personal experience. It was not merely that Jesus was like God, but that he actually was God.

These, then, are the ways in which God has revealed himself. But what happens when the revelation itself is past? Once the Passover or the crossing of the Red Sea or the contest on Mount Carmel had occurred, there was the danger that its value for those who were not present might have been lost. God will not repeat an event over and over for each person who will ever live. How could it then be preserved so that it might be known and believed by everyone? It would not do simply to leave it to human memory, especially over thousands of years. It was necessary for God to take special measures to preserve it, so that everyone could learn from it. He put it into written form, the Bible. As he did so, he ensured that the men (and possibly women) who wrote the Bible did not merely put down what they had observed or heard from others. It did not depend on their memory. Rather, the Holy Spirit worked in such a way that what they wrote was exactly what God wanted recorded; in other words, what they wrote was the Word of God. This process is what we refer to as the inspiration of Scripture.

Jesus' View of Scripture

It is important to note how the New Testament writers regarded the Bible of their day, which we today term the Old Testament. Peter, for example, said that the Scriptures are not a matter of private interpretation, for prophecy did not come "by the impulse of man, but men moved by the Holy Spirit spoke from God" (2 Pet. 1:20–21). Similarly, in a speech before one hundred twenty brethren, Peter said that "the scripture had to be fulfilled, which the Holy Spirit spoke beforehand by the mouth of David" (Acts 1:16). The same idea, that God spoke by the mouth of the prophets and of David, is also found in Acts 3:18, 21; and 4:25.

It is especially important for us to notice how Jesus regarded the Bible. Consider the fact that Jesus never hesitated to correct an erroneous idea of the scribes and Pharisees, who, as has been fairly well established, held a high view of the Bible, regarding it as God's direct message. But Jesus never rebuked them for this view, for on this point they were correct. What he did rebuke and correct was their tendency to add their own human interpretations to the revealed and inspired Word of God, thus making human traditions equal to divine Scripture.

Jesus regarded every detail of the law (by which he meant the entire Old Testament Scriptures) as being from God and therefore binding for belief and practice. He said that even though heaven and earth would pass away, not one "jot" or "tittle" would pass away from the law until all had been fulfilled (Matt. 5:18 KJV). The first word here refers to the smallest letter in the Hebrew language, which is shaped much like an apostrophe. The second is a little hook which distinguishes various Hebrew letters, for example ד ("d") from ר ("r"). No matter how minute, each element is important and binding, because God has determined that it should be in the Scriptures. In fact, Jesus rested one of his arguments upon so small a detail as the Old Testament's use of a plural rather than a singular noun (John 10:34–35; cf. Ps. 82:6). Similarly, Paul made a case on the basis of a singular noun (Gal. 3:16). Other examples could be offered, but the point is sufficiently made: every detail of the Scripture, the fact that it reads this way rather than that way, is authoritative and binding; in other words, it is inspired and it is the Word of God. Sometimes, of course, the Scripture is much more detailed than at other times, but the very form of expression is exactly what God wanted written.

God's Work in and with Scripture

Some might think that the powerful influence of the Holy Spirit upon the writers of Scripture should be considered dictation. This is not the case, however, for the distinctive personality and vocabulary of different authors can be detected in their writings; one might, for example, compare Luke's Gospel with that of John. Just as a work of sculpture will have slightly different form and texture depending upon whether the sculptor works in clay, stone, or brass, so the Spirit's inspiration of different writers reflects their unique backgrounds and experiences. Yet God had already been at work in the various influences that formed their distinctive personalities.

It is good that God reduced his revelation to writing, for that enabled him to preserve his message for us in an effective fashion. There are inevitable problems when something is preserved by merely oral means over a long period of time. The parlor game in which each player retells the same story to the next person in line indicates the types of changes that can occur. Although the Jewish people were trained to remember important things that they had heard, changes would have been inevitable over a period of centuries. God made sure that this would not happen by putting his revelation in permanent written form.

Once the Word of God was reduced to writing, it carried the very same force that his words would have if he stood before us and gave commands. In the same way, when a legislative body such as Congress passes a law, the written form is as binding as if Congress stood before us and instructed us to carry it out.

It is important to observe as well the purity of God's recorded message. We stated earlier that the Bible is exactly what God wanted us to know. Since God is all-knowing, and completely honest, this means that the Bible is completely truthful and free from error in what it affirms or teaches. While in some cases the Bible does report some false statements made by humans, such as "There is no God," it does not affirm them. What the Bible is teaching in this particular context is, "The fool says in his heart, 'There is no God'" (Ps. 14:1).

One more element is necessary if the Bible is to function as our guidebook. What if we had a true and accurate instruction manual, but it was written in a foreign language which we did not know? Or what if it was in English, but we simply did not understand what it was saying? It would be of little use to us then. We must understand what the manual says. We also need to believe that it is true. So what God has done is not simply to give us the Bible, but also to give us the interpreter, the Holy Spirit. Living within us, the Spirit helps us understand the Bible and convinces us of its truth. Indeed, Jesus promised his disciples that the Holy Spirit would come to lead them (and us) into the truth. The Spirit would call to their remembrance the things which Jesus had said and would convince them of sin, righteousness, and judgment (John 16:7-11). We call this work of the Holy Spirit illumination. Through it the Bible becomes God's Word to us; it comes alive in our experience. This work of the Holy Spirit in no way contradicts what careful study of the biblical text discloses, nor is it a shortcut making such study unnecessary. The Spirit illumines our understanding, and the more knowledge we can acquire, the more he has to work with.

The Bible as the Standard of Belief and Practice

It is vital that we have a standard of belief and practice. Have you ever looked out a window of a train parked in the station and thought you were moving, when actually it was the train on the adjacent track that was moving? I had a similar experience in a self-service car wash recently. I felt my car was rolling, so I stepped down hard on the brakes, only to discover that the car was standing still; it was the wash mechanism that was moving. We simply cannot recognize or identify the truth unless we have a fixed point of reference from which to judge.

One of my favorite stories in this regard is about a pilot who was flying alone on a dark, stormy night. He felt that his shoulder harness was too tight, so he loosened it. Shortly thereafter it still seemed too tight, so he loosened it again, but without any real improvement. Then he had the presence of mind to look at the instrument panel. He was flying upside down and going in the wrong direction.

That is a suitable metaphor for the danger of relying only upon one's feelings in matters of Christian belief. Feelings can be very deceptive.

The same is true of various other claimants to religious authority. One frequently relied upon is tradition. That which has been taught by the church, especially for a long time, is thought to be true and therefore to be followed. The problem with this is that tradition may merely be something on which the church has been mistaken longer than on other matters. The belief that the world was flat was a long-standing tradition, but it was clearly erroneous, as we now know.

Some believe that reason is the authority which we should follow. We must weigh all of the claimants to truth and decide what the truth is or, better yet, discover the truth for ourselves. Now in a sense we do follow the former approach. For unless we make our choices on the basis of the flip of a coin or something similar, we evaluate by using reason. That is what I sometimes refer to as the judicial or judging role of reason. It is quite different from the legislative role, which is actually creating or discovering the truth. An analogy here is the legislative branch of our government, which creates laws, whereas the judicial role of reason is like the judicial system, which interprets laws or tells us what they mean, and determines whether they are in accordance with the Constitution. We may use our reason to investigate the Bible's meaning and to evaluate the evidence that it is the Word of God, but not to evaluate the truth of its contents, or to pick and choose among the affirmations it contains.

The problem with thinking that reason alone can be our authority is our human limitations. Because we are limited to what we know through our senses, we do not know any ultimate truths, such as the nature of God, unless he reveals himself by coming within our experience. In addition, our reason is affected adversely by sin. Because of our inherent tendency toward selfishness, we tend to evaluate positively whatever is favorable to us. How many of us think that we have been right in only half of the differences of opinion which we have had with another? The Bible tells us that the god of this world has blinded the minds of unbelievers (2 Cor. 4:4), and some of that impairment is still present with believers.

If not feelings, tradition, or reason, with what are we to measure our theological opinions and convictions? The prophet Amos had a vision in which the Lord held a plumb line in his hand (Amos 7:7–9). A weight being attached to one of its ends, a plumb line will hang at a perpendicular angle to the ground. Without such a device it may be difficult to judge whether something is vertical. Our senses play tricks on us. The Word of God is his plumb line by which we can measure and align all of our religious beliefs and practices.

Proof of the Bible's Claims

But is there any evidence that the Bible is what it claims to be, namely, the divinely revealed truth of God, rather than simply a cleverly devised human book? There are a number of characteristics of the Bible which set it apart as more than just another book, as the inspired Word of God. One of these is fulfilled prophecy, for the ability to know and predict the future is not one of the skills possessed by human beings.

Suppose you found a book written in 1950 which predicted that the explosion of an extremely powerful bomb would take place in Hiroshima, Japan, destroying many lives and much property? What would you think? Would you be impressed? Perhaps it might even be quite specific, indicating that the date would be August 6, 1945, and that the bomb would be dropped from a B-29 named *Enola Gay*. Would you be impressed then? Hardly, for anyone could have written such a statement by looking in an encyclopedia. Suppose, on the other hand, that you found a book written in 1920 that stated that sometime in the future, somewhere in the Orient, a great disaster would take place with much loss of life. That would not be too impressive either, for it is so general in nature that there was sure to be some event that would fulfil it, perhaps a hurricane or a typhoon. But if there were an account as detailed as the first one and written well before the event, then we would suspect that something more than merely human intelligence had been involved.

This is what we have in the Bible. For there is an amazing amount of fulfilled prophecy, written well before the event and sometimes giving considerable detail regarding what was to come to pass. For instance, the place of the birth of Jesus (Mic. 5:2; Matt. 2:6), the fact that at his death the soldiers did not divide his robe but cast lots for it (Ps. 22:18; John 19:24), and the amazing detail of the fall of cities such as Nineveh (Nah. 2:5–3:13). Most of these prophecies could not be fulfilled simply by some human's deciding to bring the events to pass; and in the case of the few that could, the persons who did bring them about either did not know of the prophecies or had no desire to see them fulfilled. Behind the Bible there clearly stands an all-knowing God who has revealed his truth and directed human authors to write it by the inspiring work of his Spirit.

Study Guide

Key Questions

1. The Bible is more than a record of God's revelation in the past. It is revelation itself. What one quality ensures this distinction?
2. What advantages does the written Word of God have over other forms of revelation?
3. How does illumination differ from inspiration?
4. What role does reason have in deciding what truth is? in discovering the Bible's meaning? What are its limitations as far as understanding spiritual truths is concerned?
5. Certain types of messages from God that are contained in Scripture give evidence that the Bible is not simply a cleverly devised human book. What specific kind of biblical material makes it difficult to explain away its divine inspiration?

Bible Investigation

The Bible describes for us the ways in which God has revealed himself to humans in history—both through indirect means such as dreams and visions, and through direct means such as an audible voice and miracles. Sometimes believers think their faith would greatly benefit from these same kinds of revelation today. Read Luke 16:19–31 (the parable of the rich man and Lazarus) and John 5:46–47. What do these passages tell us about our desire for supernatural revelation? What should be our highest authority concerning matters of faith and practice?

Personal Application

Realizing that Scripture was written as God revealed himself to specific individuals at specific times within specific cultural contexts should alert us to the need to become good interpreters. We have to be able to build a bridge from the meaning that the message had for the original audience to what God intends for us to understand today.

Consider the process of deciding what Scripture means and how to apply it. What is your responsibility in the process? How important are learning and applying sound principles of interpretation? What role does tradition have? What role does the Holy Spirit play?

For Further Thought

1. Just as Jesus is both fully God and fully human, the Bible is both a divine and a human book. Perhaps too often believers have ignored the human aspects for fear of somehow diminishing the divine. Consequently, the diversity in the Bible has to a large extent not been appreciated. Where can one find the human aspects of Scripture? the divine aspects?

2. The Bible is first and foremost a theological book. It was designed to teach us about God and our relationship to him. It was written in a prescientific age. Consequently, it does not describe events and causes in the scientific language of today. Knowing this, how might you respond to the accusation that the Bible cannot be considered to be literally true?

Suggested Additional Readings

Bruce, F. F. *The New Testament Documents: Are They Reliable?* Grand Rapids: Eerdmans, 1959.

Geisler, Norman L., and William E. Nix. *From God to Us: How We Got Our Bible.* Chicago: Moody, 1974.

MacArthur, John F., Jr. *Why I Trust the Bible.* Wheaton, Ill.: Victor, 1983.

Packer, J. I. *Fundamentalism and the Word of God.* Grand Rapids: Eerdmans, 1958.

3

Who's the Boss?

At the very heart of our Christian faith is the understanding of the nature of God. If the doctrine of Scripture
is the foundation of faith, then the doctrine of God is its
superstructure, within which much of the rest of what
we believe fits.

Belief in God is not unusual. Periodically, polls are
taken regarding the religious beliefs of Americans. With
just slight numerical variations, the results are always
the same. In each case over 90 percent of Americans say
they believe in God. They have faith in the existence of
some power or being higher than humans. This is "God,"
a vague term which would encompass "the force," "the
great spirit," and even "the great whatever." To believe in
God is good business and good politics. When was the
last time that any politician declared he was an atheist?
Belief in God is almost part of the American culture. But
how many people really take this belief seriously, governing their lives by what God may have to say? That is a
very different question. People who act on the basis of
what God has to say are regarded as strange and perhaps
even dangerous.

It is important to have a correct understanding
regarding the nature of God, because our belief in this

area affects so much else of what we believe. Just as a bend given to a young tree affects the direction of its growth thereafter, so our conception of God goes a long way toward determining our other beliefs.

The Attributes of God

Who is this God? We must begin by realizing that God must be God. He is the Supreme Being, the only eternal entity in the entire universe. Everything else has come into being at some point in time. Every human has been born, every plant has sprouted, every rock has come into existence, every star has a finite point of beginning somewhere in the past, but God has always been. The psalmist said, "From everlasting to everlasting thou art God" (Ps. 90:2). And Jude speaks of him as having "glory, majesty, dominion, and authority, before all time and now and for ever" (v. 25). This reflects the fact that he is the only reality that does not depend upon anything else for existence. We are reminded daily how fragile our lives are, and how dependent we are upon favorable circumstances for continued existence. We rejoice in and marvel at the ability of modern science to extend the life expectancy of human beings, but this is still only a tiny addition to a very small period of time. God, on the other hand, has the very cause of his being within him; he not only has life, but is life, and thus is the giver of existence to everyone and everything that exists.

This God is perfect. He knows everything that is, and he can do anything. When Sarah laughed at the suggestion that she would have a baby in her old age, after having been barren all her life, God responded, "Is anything too hard for the LORD?" (Gen. 18:14). When Jesus told his disciples how hard it is for a rich man to enter into the kingdom of heaven, they asked, "Who then can be saved?" His response was, "With men this is impossible, but with God all things are possible" (Matt. 19:26).

Can God do absolutely anything? This is a question

sometimes posed by skeptics. They might, for instance, ask whether God can make a rock so large he cannot lift it. No, there are some things God cannot do. He cannot lie or break his word (Heb. 6:18). He cannot sin or even be tempted to sin (James 1:13). He cannot contradict or work against himself (thus he cannot make a rock he cannot lift). But the inability to do any of these things is not a weakness, but a strength, for they are not proper objects of power, but flaws. As the chorus says, "God can do anything . . . but fail!"

All of this greatness would be a fearful thing if God were evil or cruel. Then he would use his greatness to frustrate and even torture humans. Or what if this power were possessed by an impersonal though not malicious force? We have all seen the power of nature at work; we have seen earthquakes, volcanic eruptions, tornadoes, and even severe thunderstorms destroy human property and life. The Bible makes clear, however, that this great power belongs to a person, someone who is capable of relating to us and to whom we can relate as well. He is just as much a person as is any human being; indeed, he is more personal than any of us, for his personhood is not subject to human limitations. His personhood is also accompanied by unlimited goodness of character.

God is completely truthful. It is not possible for him to lie, for that would be a contradiction of his very nature (Heb. 6:18). Because he knows everything, he can never be mistaken; and because his very nature is honesty, he will never mislead. We can trust him with anything, even our lives. Abraham was willing to trust God with that which was most precious to him, the life of his son Isaac, for he knew that God would not take advantage of him or do any unkindness to him. This is the supreme test of integrity, whether we can trust someone with our lives.

Further, God is completely loving. Indeed, John even equated him with love (1 John 4:8). God cares about and cares for his children with a persistent and pure love.

"Love" is a word that is much used and abused in our society. It frequently refers to the physical attraction between persons of the opposite sex (and sometimes of the same sex). It is sometimes thought of as a kind of gentleness that overlooks anything negative, not wanting to cause anyone any disappointment or unpleasantness. Yet the love of God is quite different. He does not love us simply for what we can do for him. He loves unselfishly, for what he can do for us.

In our day people fall into and out of love fairly easily. In the soap operas John may be madly in love with Jane today, but tune in a year later and he will be feeling the same way about Mary. If Mary proves not to measure up to what he wants, he will have no hesitation about dumping her to find someone more attractive or interesting. God is not like that. He loved us long before we were lovable, when we did not love him, but were hostile and rebellious toward him. Nor does he let us go when we disappoint him. The people of Israel were God's chosen people, his wife so to speak. Yet they proved unfaithful, going after false gods. He did not cast them away, however. Though he may have been tempted to obliterate them and give some other group a try, perhaps the Hittites or the Amorites, God remained faithful to his promise and his covenant, his marriage vow with Israel.

The love of God does not mean mere sentimentality, however. God is a heavenly father, not a heavenly grandfather. He is not indulgent. He cares enough about us to want to see us realize our highest possibilities. So he sometimes finds it necessary to discipline, just as a parent does, not because he is angry and wants to get revenge upon us, but because he wants us to become the best we can be.

God requires of us that we be perfectly pure and holy, and he has a right to do that, for he himself is perfectly holy. There is no impurity in him, no variation, no mixture of evil with good. He is totally separate from evil, totally uncorrupted by it. He always does what is right. He indeed is the good and the right.

Sometimes humans, by great effort and concentration, manage to live lives that are reasonably righteous and holy. But that, most of us find, is contrary to our natural inclinations. It is the result of a real struggle. We first have to know what is right, then we have to choose to do it, and finally we have to be able to do it. For God, however, holiness and goodness are not something that he chooses or achieves. They are the way he is. They are part of his very nature.

And there is a constancy to God. One of the sometimes disappointing, at times encouraging, things about human beings, ourselves included, is that we change. Sometimes that is very good, as when someone grows and develops in positive ways. At other times, however, the person we once knew and greatly appreciated virtually no longer exists. The individual has changed, and for the worse. Neither of these things ever happens to God. Because he is perfection, he does not need to grow and develop, and he never slides back from what he is to something less. It is a wonderful thing to know that he is perfectly constant. Every human being has ups and downs, some more serious than others. An acquaintance of mine once said he could tell by one glance whether he should even say "Good morning" to a very moody co-worker. God is not that way; he is the same forever. He could tell Moses not only, "I am the God of Abraham, Isaac, and Jacob," but also, "This is my name for ever, and thus I am to be remembered throughout all generations" (Exod. 3:15).

God is also lofty. His thoughts are not our thoughts, nor his ways our ways; for just as the heavens are high above the earth, so is his nature higher than ours (Isa. 55:8–9). Isaiah saw him as high and lifted up (6:1). These spatial images are used by the Scripture writers to convey the idea that God is not bound to the sinful ways of this earth or of the human race; and he does not have the limited understanding, or the flawed ways of thinking and acting, that we have. It is for this reason that we do not fully understand him. By the sheer limitation of one's being, the lower cannot fully understand the higher, whether we are speaking of a cat's or dog's understanding of its human master, or of a human being's understanding of God. He goes beyond this world and the laws which govern it, of which he himself is the author.

Although God is high above our best and brightest, he is not simply an aloof being. He is also close at hand. He is at work within nature. Jeremiah saw him as present everywhere within the universe (23:24). Paul told the Athenians that God is not far from any of us, for "in him we live and move and have our being" (Acts 17:28). Although we cannot reach out and touch him, he is present with us everywhere. Like radio waves which fill a room yet are unheard until we tune a radio to receive them, God is present and active everywhere, yet we can never capture him.

God as Trinity

Many things about God distinguish him from the gods of other religions, but one of the most unusual of all is the fact that God is triune. The Hebrews had as one of their most basic and important beliefs the doctrine that God is one (Deut. 6:4). In a culture in which many people worshiped multiple gods, this was a distinctive belief. It was part of what the Hebrews recited and taught to their children. There was no question that the heavenly Father is God. But in the New Testament era it became clear that Jesus also is fully God, and then even that the Holy Spirit is as well. We will in later chapters be looking at the evidence for their deity. At this point we will simply note that all three are mentioned in the baptismal formula of Matthew 28:19 ("in the name of the Father and of the Son and of the Holy Spirit") and in Paul's benediction in 2 Corinthians 13:14 ("The grace of the Lord Jesus

Christ and the love of God [the Father] and the fellowship of the Holy Spirit be with you all"). To associate any others with God the Father on this sort of basis, unless they also are God, is a form of blasphemy of the highest kind.

The doctrine of the Trinity, the teaching that God is three and one, is not explicitly stated in the Bible. As the church tried to do justice to these two concepts, namely, that God is one yet there are three who are God, it formulated this somewhat unusual doctrine. On the surface, the Trinity seems to some to be a contradiction. How can God be one and yet three? But it is a contradiction only if God is three and one at the same time and in the same respect. And this the church has always denied. Various formulas have been employed in the process; for example, God is three persons and one nature.

In addition, many analogies have been devised in an attempt to convey the meaning of the doctrine of the Trinity. None of them is fully adequate. Either they suggest that God is Father, Son, and Holy Spirit at different times (an example here is the analogy of ice, water, and steam), or they represent the three as different parts of God. Like Augustine, the fourth- and fifth-century theologian and bishop, I believe that the most helpful analogies draw from the experience of human beings, since only humans are made in God's own image and likeness. I currently use two of these analogies together. The Trinity is something like the way in which one human may have several different roles in life, for instance, citizen, employee, and father. This emphasizes the oneness. The Trinity is also something like identical triplets, who are three separate persons, but with identical genetic makeup and various similarities that we are constantly learning more about. This emphasizes the threeness of God. Now neither of these analogies is sufficient alone, and we cannot really hold both of them together; so while the problem has been narrowed somewhat, it has not been eliminated.

We may take some comfort in the fact that scientists must think of light both as waves and as bundles of energy. It cannot be both, but both concepts must be kept in view to explain the characteristics of light. Physicists assume that when they know more about light, they will be able to understand the interrelationship of these two concepts. Similarly, we must believe that when we get to heaven, the Trinity will become clear to us. At that point we probably will exclaim, "Of course! How obvious! Why couldn't we see that before?" In the meantime, we should seek to understand the Trinity as fully as we can.

A Proper Response to God

We began by saying that God is and must be God. In light of everything else we have said, he is clearly the Lord, the ruler, the supreme person in the universe. He is the highest of all beings and therefore is deserving of our total obedience and servanthood. He does not have to answer to us. Rather, it is the other way around. God does not have to please us, for who are we to make any such claim upon him?

Sometimes, I fear, we fall into what I call "inverted theology." We think that God has to serve us, to give us what we want, to please us in what he does, to measure up to our standards of what is true and what is right. Unlike Samuel, who in response to God's call said, "Speak, LORD, for your servant is listening" (1 Sam. 3:9–10 NIV), we barrage God with our requests and even demands. We seem to be saying, "Listen, Lord, your servant is speaking." But if that is the case, then he has become the servant and we are the masters. We have turned matters upside down, so that we are now on top and God is on the bottom, inferior and subservient. That, however, is impossible, for he is truly God, and will always be so, regardless of what we make him in our experience.

It is important that we see God as he really is, for there

are some strange popular misconceptions about God that are floating around in our society. J. B. Phillips described a number of them some years ago in a delightful little book entitled *Your God Is Too Small*. Sometimes we think of God as a heavenly policeman, a celestial highway patrolman operating a speed trap, just waiting for us to violate the law so that he can hand out a ticket and see us punished or fined. This is a God who enjoys punishing people. Sometimes we go to the opposite extreme. Here God is an easygoing, indulgent person who, like an overly permissive parent or teacher, does not want to discipline anyone and lets sins slip by. But that is not God either. Sometimes we think of him as being an old man who lived in biblical times. Dressed in white robes and wearing a long beard, he may have been capable of understanding the problems of a society where people traveled by foot or on donkey or camel. But he is not capable of understanding the complexity of our modern, highly competitive society with its jet travel, satellite communications, and fax machines. Make no mistake about it, however. The fact that God understood society a long time ago does not mean he is out of touch with the present, for he has always known, from all eternity, the things that are happening now, and the things that are going to happen in the future. In fact, he planned them.

How, then, should we conceive of this great and good God? And how should we respond to him in view of who and what he is? We certainly need to make him the center of our lives just as he is, in fact, the center of the universe. We can be sure that he knows everything, and that he never leaves us, for he is everywhere. He is not restricted to the church we attend. If we move to another part of the country, we do not leave him behind, nor does he leave us. He can do anything that is a proper object of his power, so that there is never anything that he must give up on. And he is a loving God who continues to care about us even when we rebel and reject him.

A God like this deserves our worship. If you were invited for a personal visit with the president (or your favorite athlete, musician, or other hero or heroine), you would consider it a privilege, wouldn't you? You certainly wouldn't decline the invitation. And in his presence you would certainly listen respectfully to everything he had to say; you wouldn't whisper to a friend who came with you, or think about what you are going to do when you leave. You would treat him with respect. That is how we should worship God. Yet we are not to be afraid or terrified of him. He is a good, gracious, and kindly God, and we know him as our Father. We can come to him the way children come to their father or mother—without fear, and with their concerns and requests.

In our relationship with God we must keep in balance, on the one hand, respect and reverence because of what and who he is and, on the other, trust and loving warmth. To overemphasize either at the expense of the other is a serious mistake. We will boldly approach our heavenly Father, but we will always remember, too, that he is the Father and we are the children. During my undergraduate days I worked as a night attendant in a funeral home. The relationship with my employer was a warm, informal, and friendly one. Any employee who was unable to go home for Thanksgiving or Christmas was invited to his home for dinner. It was an almost ideal working relationship. But I never forgot that he was the employer and I was the employee. In professional situations I never addressed him by his first name, nor did I ever suggest that he do one of my jobs for me. While we know that God loves us, we must also always bear in mind the respect he deserves as our Father.

When we pause to think of the greatness and goodness of God, and the privilege he has given us of being his children, it is truly awe-inspiring. We cannot help but join in singing:

O Lord my God! When I in awesome wonder
Consider all the worlds Thy hands have made,
I see the stars, I hear the rolling thunder,
Thy power throughout the universe displayed.

And when I think that God, His Son not sparing,
Sent Him to die, I scarce can take it in;
That on the cross, my burden gladly bearing,
He bled and died to take away my sin.

Then sings my soul, my Savior God, to Thee:
How great Thou art! How great Thou art!
Then sings my soul, my Savior God, to Thee:
How great Thou art! How great Thou art!

(Stuart K. Hine, 1953)

Study Guide

Key Questions

1. Why is our understanding of the nature of God so crucial to our belief system?
2. How might you describe (but not fully explain) the concept of the Trinity to a child of elementary-school age?
3. Are we sometimes guilty of "inverted theology," especially in our prayer lives?
4. In view of who and what God is, how should we respond to him?

Bible Investigation

1. God is truly bigger than we can imagine. Sometimes we presumptuously assume that God cannot act unless we allow him to. Read the story of Balak and Balaam in Numbers 22–24. How does this passage teach us that God can accomplish his will even without our cooperation?
2. Sometimes people see the God of the Old Testament as a demanding, quick-tempered judge, and the God of the New Testament as a patient, merciful father. It's important to remember that God is not schizophrenic, nor does he at any time change his nature. Using a Bible concordance, check to see how often the Old Testament uses words like "gracious," "compassionate," "slow to anger," "loving," "kind," and "merciful" to describe God.

Personal Application

Knowing the attributes of God—what he is really like—should make a difference in our lives. Complete the following statements to show how the various attributes of God as revealed by the Bible affect your life. The first one will serve as an example:

Because God is eternal . . .

> he is the giver of life to everyone and everything that exists. Consequently, I am totally dependent on him.

Because God is all-knowing and all-powerful . . . .

Because God is personal . . . .

Because God is completely truthful . . . .

Because God is completely loving . . . .

Because God is good . . . .

Because God is perfectly holy . . . .

Because God is unchanging . . . .

Because God is just . . . .

For Further Thought

Think back to the concept of God that you had as you were growing up. Did you think of him as either a celestial highway patrolman or an indulgent grandfather? How has your concept of God changed over the years? What contributed to those changes?

Another conception of God sees him as a cosmic chess player. In one variation of this conception, God moves all the pieces in the game, and humans have little choice in determining their own destinies. In another variation, God's moves are dependent upon the moves that a human makes. Describe a situation in which you may have viewed God in one of these ways. What is fundamentally wrong with each of these views?

Suggested Additional Readings

Beisner, E. Calvin. *God in Three Persons*. Wheaton, Ill.: Tyndale, 1984.

Benson, Clarence H. *The Triune God*. Wheaton, Ill.: Evangelical Teacher Training Association, 1970.

Humphreys, Fisher. *The Nature of God*. Nashville: Broadman, 1985.

Phillips, J. B. *Your God Is Too Small.* New York: Walker, 1979.

Sproul, R. C. *The Holiness of God.* Wheaton, Ill.: Tyndale, 1985.

Strauss, Richard L. *The Joy of Knowing God.* Neptune, N.J.: Loizeaux, 1984.

4

What's Going On Around Here?

In the preceding chapter, we described what God is like. We observed something of his wisdom and power. God would have possessed these attributes even if he had never done anything, but his moral qualities, such as love and faithfulness, would have been expressed only internally, within the Trinity, that is, in relationships between the Father, Son, and Holy Spirit, because in the beginning there was only God. Nothing else existed but God himself. For whatever reasons, known only fragmentarily to us, God decided to bring into existence something other than himself. God did not change in his being or what he is, but in his doing, or what he does. For he is an active, dynamic being, whose qualities of greatness and goodness are expressed continuously.

Before we examine what God does, however, it is important to observe that God plans. What he has done and is doing and will do he has planned from all eternity. His actions are no mere haphazard workings, last-minute deeds, or reflex reactions. Whether we have in view historical events affecting nations (Isa. 37:26; Acts 17:26), the redemptive work of Christ (Eph. 1:11–12), or the choice of a particular person for a special position of service, what God has done is the execution of decisions made by the Triune God.

God's Original Work of Creation

The first thing that God did was to create. Without using any preexisting materials, God brought into being all that is, the heavens with the stars and planets, the earth and all of its inanimate nature, and every living thing, including the angels in heaven. The Bible begins with this solemn pronouncement: "In the beginning God created the heavens and the earth" (Gen. 1:1). For the Hebrews, "heavens and the earth" was an expression for "everything that is."

This work of creation was different from anything that you or I do as humans. If I want to build a cabinet, I must go to the lumberyard and purchase the lumber. If I want to bake a cake, I must go to the grocery store and purchase the ingredients. I can make things, but only out of what already exists. But God did not merely make, he created! He brought into existence the very building materials of the universe, their physical substance and all that is. This was not a case of God's fashioning whatever he found into something else, as the gods of some other religions are believed by their followers to have done, nor of making something by an outpouring of his own nature, but a genuine bringing into being of that which did not exist before. He did not have the use of any materials already in existence. Thus, everything that is or has been owes its existence to him.

This is not to say that God directly created at the beginning everything that has ever existed. He began the process, providing the raw materials out of which have come succeeding generations of plants, animals, and humans. And humans have been given the knowledge and wisdom to make new substances and forms from what God has provided. This, however, is also God's work.

He created originally, and he is continuing to make from that original creation additional entities.

The Bible does not tell us just how long ago or over how long a period of time God carried out his work of creating. While some, such as Archbishop James Ussher, have attempted to determine the dates of the early events of the Bible by adding together the years between the various generations listed in the genealogies, we now know from closer examination that the genealogies were not intended to be used that way. Further, although the creation account in Genesis 1 describes God as creating in six days, the Hebrew word for "day" is a general one which can be used of a twenty-four-hour period or of longer periods of time, much as we today use phrases like "in those days." The exact time is not of great importance to us, for creation is no more supernatural for being slow or rapid. Peter tells us that with God one day is as a thousand years, and a thousand years as one day (2 Pet. 3:8).

God's work of creation means that all of what we find in our world derives directly or indirectly from God. In a very real sense, it is his, and we should be thankful to him for his goodness and generosity in making it available to us. This also means that we should show proper concern for it. The various components of the creation were provided for the human to sustain life. We are not the only part of the creation that is valuable to God, however. Jesus said that God watches over the birds of the air (Matt. 10:29), and God spared Nineveh because of the people and cattle there (Jon. 4:11). So ecological concerns should be important to us, for they relate to the precious creation which God has produced.

God's Subsequent Work with Creation

It is important to remember that God did not merely create the universe and then leave it to operate without his supervision. That is not the Christian God, but rather the god of the deists, who compare him to an artisan who makes a watch, winds it, and then leaves it to run on its own. Such a god, unlike the God of the Old and New Testaments, is indifferent to the fortunes of the members of his creation.

God preserves his creation in existence. In the prayer of confession led by Ezra and the Levites, the people of Israel acknowledge that God continues to maintain his creation (Neh. 9:6); and Paul tells us that in Christ all things "hold together" (Col. 1:17). We have already noted that God preserves the birds of the air (Matt. 10:29), and there are innumerable statements, especially in the Psalms (e.g., 91), about God's preserving his people. Vivid examples are found in the Book of Daniel, where Daniel is spared in the den of lions, and Shadrach, Meshach, and Abednego are kept alive in the fiery furnace.

God also is at work governing what happens within his creation, so that what he has planned and chosen comes about. God even affects what happens in the ordinary course of nature. Jesus said the sunshine and the rain are sent by the Father (Matt. 5:45). He is in control of history, governing who comes to power and who falls, and when (Dan. 4:24–25). Our individual abilities and circumstances are God's doing as well (1 Cor. 4:6–7). All actions, even those of sinful humans, are depicted as being under the control of God. Thus the actions of unbelieving rulers such as Cyrus are part of the divine plan. In fact, Cyrus is described as the Lord's "shepherd" (Isa. 44:28) and his "anointed" (Isa. 45:1). While God does not cause evil actions, he wills to permit them and then utilizes them for good.

Much of the care God exercises over the universe is of a regular kind, including working through the processes of nature and so-called natural laws. We may not even be aware of the divine working. Taking a different route and thus avoiding involvement in an accident, and not becoming infected by a given disease, are examples. We often take this type of thing for granted. There are other times, however, when God's working is of a more extraordinary type. This is what we sometimes refer to as miracles. They are events for which no natural laws can account. It is not that they break the laws of nature, but that God introduces a supernatural force sufficient to counteract the laws of nature. Say I drop a book three times and it falls to the floor. Then I drop it again, but this time it does not fall because my other hand is beneath it. The law of gravity is still operating upon the book, but my hand negates the effect by pushing upward on the book. In like manner, God does not suspend the laws of nature when he makes an axhead float, or raises someone from the dead, but he introduces supernatural forces which negate their effect. These supernatural forces are powerful witnesses to the presence and action of God, since they are unexplainable in human terms.

God's Agents

As God's followers, we are his agents. He has given us the task of caring for the creation (Gen. 1:26, 28), of proclaiming his message of salvation (Matt. 28:18–20), and of ministering love in his name (Mark 9:41). He has chosen to work in partnership with us. This partnership entails prayer. God has so designed the world and limited himself that he will work certain matters only when we communicate to him our desire for them to come about. Contrary to what is sometimes thought, prayer is not getting God to change his will to agree with our will, but declaring our strong commitment to the carrying out of his will.

God also has special agents called angels who carry out his will within his creation. We sometimes make one of two opposite errors regarding angels. We may either virtually disbelieve in them, at least in practice, or we may attribute everything to them.

Actually, we are told very little in the Bible about the origin of angels except that they apparently were created prior to human beings, and had a one-time opportunity to choose obedience or disobedience of God. Some chose to obey, and were confirmed in their obedience and goodness. They now serve to carry out God's will in the world. Others, however, led by Satan, or the devil, disobeyed, fell, and became the evil opponents of God (Jude 6).

The good angels serve several roles in God's economy: they continually praise and glorify God (Ps. 103:20; Luke 2:13–14), minister to believers (Ps. 34:7; Acts 12:6–11), execute judgment upon God's enemies (Exod. 14:19–20; 2 Kings 19:35), and will be involved in Christ's second coming (Matt. 13:39–42; 24:31). They are important servants of God. They are higher in intelligence and power than human beings, but they are still limited, finite beings subject to God's control and will. They are to be respected, but never worshiped, by human beings.

The Problem of Evil

One very major problem faces us when we think of God as being in control of the world. This is the problem of evil, which often is put in the form of the question, "Why do bad things happen to good people?" This is a very real problem, and it is more than just an intellectual issue. If we are not currently experiencing it, we will sooner or later. It takes two forms. One is what we sometimes call natural evil, destructive occurrences within nature such as tornadoes, earthquakes, volcanic eruptions, and diseases like cancer. The other form is moral evil, the evil things done by human beings, especially to other human beings. The problem can be expressed quite simply, although the solution certainly cannot: If God is all-powerful, he would be able to prevent evil; if he is loving, he would want to prevent evil; yet there is evil in the world.

This is perhaps the most difficult of all problems for Christianity or any religion which believes in a powerful and good God, for the presence of evil is undeniable. One has only to read the daily newspaper or watch the evening news on television to verify this. Christianity's greatest theologians have sought to deal with the problem, but it remains with us. While we cannot resolve it completely, certain themes of the biblical teaching serve to alleviate it somewhat.

One thing that must be borne in mind is that evil in general is a result of sin in general. When Adam and Eve sinned, a whole host of ills entered the world (Gen. 3:16–19). That we all live in this fallen world means that ill may come upon someone who is not personally responsible for any sin. Beyond that, however, specific sins may be the cause of specific evils coming into an individual's life (Josh. 7:24–25; Gal. 6:7–8), although this principle should be invoked cautiously. On the other hand, what seems to be evil may, in the long run, turn out to be quite different, for God sometimes uses apparent evil to accomplish good, as in the case of Joseph (Gen. 45:5–8; 50:20). We should also observe that God has taken the effects of sin upon himself. Through his life, death, and resurrection, Jesus Christ has overcome sin and evil. Finally, Christianity has never claimed that there will be perfect justice within this life, but, rather, that this life is not the whole of reality. There are a coming judgment, when justice will be administered, and a heaven and a hell.

God's Judgment

God's final work in this world will be one of judgment. At times it appears that evil is unpunished and good unrewarded. Yet, even within history, God is at work passing judgment upon human belief and conduct, and frequently executing that judgment. Consider, for example, the captivity of Israel and Judah, the just deserts of their wickedness. Similarly, the judgments on Sodom and Gomorrah (Gen. 19), Nebuchadnezzar (Dan. 4) and Belshazzar (Dan. 5), and Herod (Acts 12:21–23) were evidences of God's ruling righteously. And then there is a great final judgment coming, when God will judge us all in terms of our faithfulness and obedience (Matt. 24–25).

God sets high standards for us, and is sometimes quite stringent in what he requires of us, because he wants us to become the very best we can be for him. Sometimes he has to discipline us, but more often we should think of him as encouraging us and rejoicing in the good in our lives. But whether he encourages or corrects us, he does so because there will one day be that great final examination, and he wants us to be well prepared for it (Heb. 12:5–11).

Over the years that I have been a private pilot, I have flown with many different flight instructors and examiners, first in the process of acquiring my license, and later in checkouts for specific aircraft and in the required biennial flight review. Some instructors are good at making one fly poorly. I recall one in particular who delighted in catching me in an error and would pounce on it, as if to say, "Aha! I caught you!" And of course, that reaction frequently led to my making another mistake. Other instructors, however, have a gift for making one fly well. I was fortunate in having one such instructor in my primary flight training. Pat would always find something good to commend me for in each day's session. Sometimes he would say, "Any landing you can walk away from is a good landing," at a time when I needed to hear that. Other instructors would scream at a student and grab the controls when a mistake was made. But unless he thought I was going to injure us or damage the aircraft, Pat would let me make the mistake, and then he would smile and say, "I'll bet you won't do that again!" But as the time of training drew toward the end, Pat became much more intolerant. Instead of the permitted fifty feet of altitude deviation, he would bark at me if I strayed off by ten feet. I remember thinking, "He has really become a grouch!" Why he did that I understood better the day of my official check flight for the Federal Aviation Administration. Pat's greater demands enabled me to pass that examination with a margin for error. God's judgment and discipline, when they come, are intended to prepare us for a time of glorious reward.

A Proper Response to God's Work

We have seen that God is the Lord of all of history. He is the one who began it. That is the doctrine of creation. He is the one who has been and is and will be in control of this universe throughout all time. That is the doctrine of providence. He is also the one who will cause history to fulfil all he has planned for it, and will then bring it to its end. That is judgment.

This, then, is the biblical picture of God: the loving father, the caring shepherd, who watches over us with concern for our welfare, and who is in control of everything that he has created. In light of this picture, what should be our reaction as believers? How should these great truths about God affect how we live? In the final analysis, coming up with answers to such questions is the purpose for the study of doctrine.

1. Because the whole universe has been created by God and belongs to him, we should regard it with great respect and treat it carefully and lovingly, as he does. Certainly we are to use it for our welfare, but we are not to abuse or exploit it. We are not the only members of the creation that have value to God. He pronounced his work "good" (Gen. 1:25) even before the creation of the human, and "very good" after he made the man (Gen. 1:31). To make sure it retains this goodness, we must exercise carefully

the responsibility he has given us as stewards of the creation. That means that ecology should deeply concern us.

2. We should have a confidence that God will protect and provide for our lives, and bring history to its intended ends. Joseph in prison in Egypt could remain calm and trusting, because he knew that God was in control of what happened, and would accomplish his will (Gen. 45:7). He is watching over us. This does not mean that he will never permit anything unpleasant to happen to us, but that he is able to use even negative circumstances to accomplish his purposes. While our immediate situation may not always be pleasant, God is working in it for our eternal good (Rom. 8:28). He is even able to bring good out of human mistakes or evil actions.

3. We should assess ourselves honestly. We should not take pride in our own accomplishments, nor demean ourselves because we do not have some of the gifts which others have. It is, after all, God who is the cause of the differences among humans (1 Cor. 4:6–7).

4. We should recognize that God works in many different ways, and that the nonmiraculous, regular actions of the universe are as much his doing as are the more spectacular events called miracles.

5. Knowing God and understanding something of his purposes, we must seize the opportunity, the responsibility, and the privilege of helping bring about his will in the world. This includes, but is not limited to, prayer.

The Christian has confidence and courage in the face of the uncertainties of life. This outlook does not stem merely from a positive mental attitude, but from knowing the God who is in charge of everything that happens throughout time. The songwriter has put it well:

> Be not dismayed whate'er betide,
> God will take care of you;
> Beneath his wings of love abide,
> God will take care of you.

Through days of toil when heart doth fail,
  God will take care of you;
When dangers fierce your path assail,
  God will take care of you.

No matter what may be the test,
  God will take care of you;
Lean, weary one, upon his breast,
  God will take care of you.

  God will take care of you,
    Through every day, o'er all the way;
  He will take care of you,
    God will take care of you.

                    (Civilla Durfee Martin, 1904)

Study Guide

Key Questions

1. The author explains that "God did not merely create the universe and then leave it to operate without his supervision." What are the primary ways in which God continuously expresses and demonstrates his greatness and goodness?
2. How does God usually exercise care over his creation? Why is it difficult for human beings to recognize this activity as divine?
3. At times God demonstrates his control over the universe in extraordinary ways. What is the relationship between this miraculous divine activity and the laws of nature?
4. In addition to governing the world through natural laws and occasional miracles, God works his will through his chosen agents. Who are these agents, and what are their responsibilities?
5. What role does prayer play in accomplishing what God has planned?

Bible Investigation

Carefully read Psalm 91, a psalm that many Christians go to for comfort and assurance in the midst of adversity. Some conclude that this passage teaches that God gives to believers some special protection from the dangers and tragedies of life. Sometimes, however, Christians suffer as much as or even more sickness, pain, sorrow, and death than do non-Christians. Perhaps a careful look at this psalm can resolve this apparent contradiction.

Does the psalm really assume that believers will not experience "trouble" (v. 15)? If not "trouble," what is it that believers will be saved from (v. 3)? What will they observe (v. 8)? What exactly will the angels have charge over (vv. 11–13)? In what crucial "way" will believers be guarded? (In this passage, the word *ways* refers to a person's actions and behavior, not to such things as illnesses, disappointments, sorrow, and death.) Whom does God ultimately deliver (v. 14)? How does one actually demonstrate this kind of love toward God (see 1 John 5:3)? By now you should have a fairly clear concept of the nature of God's protection as well as its special benefits.

Personal Application

Some Christians live a fretful existence trying constantly to determine the will of God for their lives in every given situation. In order to please God, they feel compelled to discover the one best course of action which will put them at the very center of his will.

It is important to remember that while human actions are under God's control, he exercises that control by utilizing human freedom of choice in decision making. That is why God can hold us accountable for our choices. We should also bear in mind that God is fully capable of accomplishing his good will, even when what he wishes for us may be somewhat different from what we choose.

How can a believer please God in making major decisions, such as whether or not to marry, take a new job, or begin a new ministry? Can there be more than one "best" course of action? Under what circumstances does a wrong choice place a believer outside of God's will? In general, on what basis should a Christian make decisions in areas where the Bible gives no specific command or principle? See Ephesians 5:15–21.

For Further Thought

At times we human beings attempt to understand and explain God's providential activity. Even a prophet of God like Habakkuk can have many questions. What was his specific complaint (1:1–4)?

When God answered that he was going to send the Babylonians to judge and punish Judah, Habakkuk had yet another question: How could God use the more wicked to bring judgment on his chosen people, the "more righteous"? How did God answer this question (see ch. 2, especially vv. 4, 16–17)?

In what ways is the present situation similar to the world in which Habakkuk lived (see 1:1–4)? How well does Habakkuk articulate the inner struggles of contemporary individuals who try to understand God's workings?

Habakkuk was convinced of God's certain and universal judgment. Read chapter 3 and summarize his response to this knowledge. How can this response help shape our own response to this aspect of God's providence?

Suggested Additional Readings

Geisler, Norman L. *Knowing the Truth About Creation.* Ann Arbor: Servant, 1989.

Lewis, C. S. *Miracles.* New York: Macmillan, 1978.

———. *The Problem of Pain.* New York: Macmillan, 1978.

Sproul, R. C. *God's Will and the Christian.* Wheaton, Ill.: Tyndale, 1986.

5

Who Am I?

During the late 1960s, when I was teaching college undergraduates, the big issue for many of them was the identity crisis. They were seeking to find out "who they were." I facetiously suggested that the solution was simply to issue all of them name tags, which they could wear upside down on their chests. Then they could look down and immediately see who they were. That, of course, did not answer their question. They were not asking merely for their name, but for their identity, seeking to determine who and what they were in this world. For college students, suspended somewhere between adolescence and adulthood, that was not an easy question to answer.

What do you say when someone asks who you are? Do you simply give your name, perhaps your address, and in certain circumstances your social-security number? To the automatic teller machine the most important part of your identity is your personal identification number, without which it will not dispense cash from your account. Often we answer the question, "But who are you really?" by indicating what we do, our occupation, or perhaps our role relative to the person asking. In some societies the question is answered by specifying the tribe or family that one belongs to. Philosophically oriented persons may answer in terms of where they believe the human race came from and where it is going. The answer to the question is very important, for what we think about ourselves will greatly affect how we live.

Human Beings as Creatures of God

The people who know us best can better answer the question of who we are than can strangers or mere acquaintances. For the Christian, the person who knows us best is not our spouse, parent, son, or daughter, but our heavenly Father, God. In the Bible we find the most penetrating answers to the question of who we are.

The Bible tells us first that we are creatures, brought into existence by the will of God. In the Book of Genesis, we are told that God made man from the dust of the earth, probably a reference to the most basic building blocks of the known universe. He did not make Adam from any previously existing form of life, but brought the entirety of his nature into being.

This is a reminder of a number of things. We are limited beings. As great as humans are, as wondrous and valuable, we are still creatures, with a point of beginning in time and dependence upon the Maker. We therefore are subject to God. We are not in a position to put ourselves at the center of the universe. We also have some things in common with the other creatures. Like them, we have come from God's hand. The other creatures are thus our distant cousins, and this kinship should affect how we regard them and treat them. Although there is a great difference between us and them, the greatest difference lies between God on the one hand, and us and the rest of the creation on the other. There is only one God. Our commonality with the other creatures means that we are subject to many of the same laws and have many of the same needs that they have. Our creaturehood, our limitations, are not something to be ashamed of, but to be accepted, while we strive to develop ourselves to our fullest potential.

The Image of God

It is important to notice the unique place of humans within the creation. The man was the very last and thus the highest of God's creations. Further, the man is characterized differently from the other creatures. Only of the humans is it said that God created them in his own image and likeness (Gen. 1:26–27), in other words, like God himself. In a sense, God used himself as the pattern in making us. That thought is breathtaking.

To some extent, we humans partake of the unlimited qualities of God, and thus are not as limited as the animals are. Animals can live only in the present and in their location within the created world. While we also are located in the here and now, we can rise above it. Memory enables us to relive the past. Imagination enables us to anticipate the future, and thus live partly in it. We can envision ourselves somewhere else, especially places where we have been before. We have powers of reasoning and of language which enable us to communicate and accumulate culture. We have personality, which enables us to relate to other human beings.

Most important of all is that our special endowment from God enables us to relate to him. Of all of the creatures, only the human has the privilege of communing consciously with him, as depicted by God's coming to walk with Adam and Eve in the Garden of Eden. It was apparent that they had been created to serve God, for they were immediately assigned the task of having dominion over the creation, which began with Adam's naming the animals.

Another distinguishing characteristic of humans is their eternality. Every other creature comes into existence, lives, and dies, and that is the end of it. It decomposes or is consumed by some other creature—its existence ends at death. This is not true of humans, however. Although we all have a point of beginning in time and space, death is not our end. We continue to live on, eternally, either with

God or apart from God. Our earthly life is only a small part of our total existence. In light of our unending existence, Jesus, Paul, and others emphasized that we should conduct our life here wisely. Realizing our eternality puts a different perspective upon life and should affect the way we conduct ourselves, for unlike the other creatures we will not simply die and fade away.

It is important to understand that in a sense the image of God is not something which humans possess, but something which they are. That means that the whole person is the image of God. Sometimes Christians have thought otherwise. They have thought that some specific portion or aspect of human nature constitutes or contains God's image, and that we must therefore develop this one aspect to the neglect or even suppression of the others. For example, some Christians concentrate on intellectual development to the neglect of the condition of the body. Now to be sure, reason is something humans do not share with other creatures, whereas the body is something that they do share. We need to understand and remember, however, that basically the human is a unitary being, not a composite of parts, and that the entire person is in the image of God. Thus care for our body is important, for it is part of what we are and affects the whole of our being.

Human Purpose and Value

We can find our real significance by fulfilling the purpose for which we were created. There is a sense in which the ancient philosopher Aristotle was right when he said that something that does not fulfil its destiny, or serve the role for which it was intended, is not really what it is. I am reminded here of the thick telephone directories we had when we were living in Chicago. Two of them, placed on a chair, served very well for a small child to sit on. They in effect converted a regular chair into a high chair. But in that situation the telephone book was not really a telephone book. It was not fulfilling its highest end, that for which it was intended. Any object of similar thickness would have served just as well. Similarly, a telephone can be used as a paperweight or a bookend, but it is then not what it really is.

To apply this analogy to ourselves: we are less than fully human, less than our highest and best, if we are not fulfilling the purpose for which we were created. Some current conceptions of human nature are flattering until we realize how far short they fall of the truth that we are created in the image of God. Some philosophies, including political philosophies, regard humans as basically animals. If their fundamental needs of physical sustenance and pleasure are met, it is argued, people will be satisfied and happy. Perhaps, because of their greater complexity, humans will need more amusement and recreation than will animals, but that is a difference only of degree. Any attempt to live only in terms of satisfying such needs will necessarily lead to disappointment and frustration, for the basic human purpose is not being realized.

I once served as interim pastor of a church in a very wealthy suburb. One of the members of the congregation was a domestic servant. When someone commented on the lavish estates, with their beautiful and spacious grounds surrounded by high fences and gates, he responded, "But there is a lot of unhappiness behind those walls." John D. Rockefeller reportedly was once asked, "How much money does it take to satisfy a man?" He replied, "Just a little bit more." Augustine had tried all the pleasures of life, even the intellectual pleasures, but found that "the heart is restless for God, and it cannot find rest until it finds it in you, O God."

The fact that we were created by God gives us purpose and great value. It is not that we are part of God, or that part of him was used to make us, but that we have been made in such a way that we resemble him. We hear a great deal these days about self-esteem and its importance to our happiness. Accordingly, many persons attempt to increase their own self-esteem (and that of others) in a direct way; they pump themselves up, so to speak. There is a problem with that, however. The person who is below average in virtually every way will of course be made to feel inferior. This is to disregard a most important fact which confers infinite value upon every human being: each of us is made by God in his own image and likeness. Nothing, not social class, education, economic status, race, or anything else, changes that fact.

It helps our self-understanding to know where we came from. Suppose that you learned that you were descended from royalty, or from some famous musician or scholar. Would that affect your self-understanding? I believe it would. Unlike the evolutionist, Christians understand that it is not because some impersonal natural forces produced them that they are what they are. We did not come into being, nor take on our individual form and characteristics, because of impersonal, unconscious forces lower than ourselves. Rather, our value is conferred upon us from above, by a wise and good God who chose to make us in his image.

We are the highest of God's creatures, the most valuable to him. This is demonstrated in several ways in Scripture. Noting the disciples' anxiety about themselves, Jesus reassured them by pointing out that nothing can happen to a sparrow without the Father's knowledge and permission (Matt. 10:29–31). He then reminded them that they were of more value than many sparrows. He also pointed out that God even knows the number of hairs on our heads (v. 30), not a particularly significant piece of information, but indicative of the completeness of God's knowledge of us and our circumstances. If someone as important as the eternal, all-powerful Creator of everything that is pays that sort of attention to us, we must be of great value indeed.

Dominion and Freedom

We noted earlier that God assigned to humans dominion over the rest of creation. This was one of the consequences which followed from their being created in his own image. It was God's intention that humankind would carry out his work in his world, which was originally identified with tending the Garden of Eden, but which actually meant caring for the entire world which he had created. We are, as Adam and Eve's descendants, charged with that same responsibility of caring for the creation, using it to meet our own needs, but also protecting it, and developing it as God himself would do. This means understanding and controlling the creation, beginning of course with one's own self. Thus all studies of the creation (i.e., all learning) are appropriate.

Part of exercising dominion involves controlling oneself, and thus being genuinely free, so that one may freely serve and obey God. If we fully understand the doctrine of humanity, we will be careful to avoid falling into practices or associations which deprive us of that freedom. This may even mean care in managing one's resources so that one's options are not foreclosed, and it certainly means avoiding any sort of addictive behavior or substance.

But can we really be free if we have committed ourselves to following and obeying God? Is this not a terrible restriction upon our initiative and choice? That is how Christianity appears to some people. In reality, however, true freedom is not the ability or the opportunity to do absolutely anything whatsoever. Such is not freedom, but anarchy. It can be very self-destructive, a form of slavery to oneself. True freedom is the ability to do and become that which the Creator intended us to do and be. Following the pattern he has laid down does not restrict, but enables us to realize our potential.

Years ago, I decided the time had come to learn to play

golf, so I enrolled in an evening course in beginning golf at the University of Minnesota. I found that the instructor was very strict about what he would let us do and how we could swing a club. We had to stand in a certain way, grip the golf club in a certain way, keep our heads down and left arm straight, and so on. There were times when I tired of this restrictive routine. I felt like shouting, "I just want to swing the club however I feel like swinging it. I want to be free." If I had done that, however, I would have been free to hit the ball into the rough, the water hazard, the sand trap. By restricting how I exercised my freedom, I became free to hit the ball straight and far down the middle of the fairway. Just as a railroad locomotive that tired of always running on the tracks and started out on a more creative route would bog down, so persons who try to exercise their freedom independently of God or contrary to his will find that slavery rather than freedom is the result.

The Universality of the Image of God

It is important to see that the image of God not only gives us value, but it also gives value to every human being. For all humans are in the image of God. Adam was an individual to be sure, but he was also the entire human race, and his very name means "human." Thus, when he and Eve were created in God's image, it was all human beings who were thus endowed. It is worth observing, also, that the parallelism of Genesis 1:27 makes clear that Eve was made in the divine image and likeness just as much as was Adam. And although all of humanity fell into sin so that to some extent the image was damaged or marred, yet it is clear that the image has not been lost. For in Genesis 9:6, long after the fall, murder is prohibited on the grounds that the human is in God's image. This means that killing a human being is in a sense an attack upon God himself, and that we should have the same respect for other humans that God has for them. Certainly the taking of a human life should be something abhorrent to us. There may be times when it is right to kill another human, as in self-defense, but that will never be a genuine good, but only the lesser of two evils in a world in which, because of the presence of sin, the best and perfect cannot always be attained.

In addition to sparing human life, we will be concerned to prevent whatever may make it difficult or painful. As believers we will want to do all we can to ensure genuine freedom for all persons. The right and responsibility to exercise dominion was given to all humans, not just to some. Thus it is not right that one human should exercise dominion over others in such a way as to take away their capacity to exercise dominion. This is not to say that authority should not be given to publicly elected and appointed civil servants. It does mean, however, that any form of enslavement is wrong. The recent thrusts toward greater political freedom in our world are therefore encouraging. Every human person has a dignity which has been conferred by the Creator and which we should strive to preserve and develop. No matter how uneducated and uncultured, unkempt and unclean, vile and coarse, wicked and immoral, every person is something wonderful and of importance to God; for he has made all of us in his own image. Even the unbeliever, resisting and blaspheming God, does so by (mis)using the powers of personality which were received from the Creator.

That every person experience salvation is also an object of God's concern. Everyone was made to have fellowship with God, a goal which sin prevents or impedes. God, however, "is patient . . . , not wanting anyone to perish, but everyone to come to repentance" (2 Pet. 3:9 NIV). We therefore must be concerned about the evangelization of every human being, for in so doing we will be helping bring about in their lives the purpose for which God gave them existence.

A Proper Response to the Doctrine of Humanity

If we have correctly understood what the Bible tells us about humanity, certain consequences follow:

1. We will have a proper self-esteem, realizing that our value has been conferred upon us by God himself.

2. We will seek to fellowship with, worship, and obey God, realizing that, as the Westminster Shorter Catechism puts it, "the chief end of man is to glorify God and enjoy him forever."

3. We will seek to exercise good stewardship in the management of God's creation, attempting to bring it to the goals God has in view.

4. We will realize the value of every human being and treat each one with respect and dignity. We will seek to preserve and promote each individual's freedom, right to exercise dominion, and welfare. We will especially seek, through the announcement of the Good News, to bring all persons to the fellowship with God for which they were created.

5. We will treat the whole of our human nature with respect and seek to develop the good in every regard—physical, psychological, and spiritual.

Study Guide

Key Questions

1. To what extent does one's self-concept affect how one lives?
2. Describe some of the things that human beings have in common with the other creatures. What one quality does humankind possess that is unique? What special endowments does this quality entail?
3. Aristotle said that the real meaning of something is found when it fulfils the purpose for which it was intended. What does Scripture teach is the primary purpose for the existence of human beings?
4. Make a list of some of the ways in which people in contemporary society have attempted to find fulfilment. How do you explain the failure of these pursuits to prevent disappointment and frustration?
5. What one overriding responsibility was humankind given from the time of creation? What implications does this mandate have for the protection of our environment? our bodies? those who are unable to care for themselves?
6. What is the nature of true freedom? How can one become genuinely free?

Bible Investigation

Read both Psalm 8 and Psalm 139 in their entirety. Both of these psalms exalt various attributes of God; they also point out the unique role and relationship with God that human beings have been given since creation. What is the basis for the special value and privileged position God confers on human beings? How do you reconcile Psalm 8:5 with Isaiah 2:22 and 64:6? What response should a proper understanding of ourselves bring? See especially Psalm 8:9; Psalm 139:6, 14, 17–18, 23–24.

Personal Application

1. There are many seminars and workshops these days that aim to help the participants elevate their self-

esteem. What is potentially good about such classes? What are the inherent limitations?

2. "Eat, drink, and be merry, for tomorrow you shall die." "Go for it. You only live once!" "Life is uncertain. Eat dessert first!" What is intrinsically wrong with these philosophies? What distinguishing characteristic of humanity don't they take into account?

3. Many people see the essence of humanity as having a free will to be able to make free choices. They see freedom primarily in terms of a lack of restraint. In what situations can this concept of freedom actually lead to slavery? How would you explain to a teenager that the Ten Commandments are designed to ensure one's freedom?

For Further Thought

"As believers we will want to do all we can to ensure genuine freedom for all persons. . . . No matter how uneducated and uncultured, unkempt and unclean, vile and coarse, wicked and immoral, every person is something wonderful and of importance to God, for he has made all of us in his own image." How does this understanding of humanity affect our attitude and approach toward the elderly? the institutionalized? the homeless? welfare recipients? minority groups? oppressive foreign governments? people with AIDS?

Suggested Additional Readings

McDonald, H. D. *The Christian View of Man.* Westchester, Ill.: Crossway, 1981.

Machen, J. Gresham. *The Christian View of Man.* Carlisle, Pa.: Banner of Truth, n.d.

Packer, J. I. *Knowing Man.* Westchester, Ill.: Crossway, 1979.

Whatever Became of Sin?

Several years ago, a noted psychiatrist, Karl Menninger, wrote a book entitled *Whatever Became of Sin?* The title served to call attention to the fact that sin is not a prominent word in the vocabulary of today. It is not that sin has declined, but that it just is not called by that name anymore. Ours is an age which wants to have an easy conscience, and admitting to sin, to moral and spiritual wrongdoing, is not the way to achieve it.

The fact is, however, that most of us are very familiar with the reality of sin, whether we call it that or not. "Are you speaking on sin at your church this Sunday night?" asked a friend. "Why are you doing that? We're all experts on that subject already." Although many people don't know or believe a lot about the Bible, about God, about Jesus Christ, everyone knows something about sin. It is easy to observe, for it is all around us. More than that, however, it is something that all of us experience personally. The Bible says, "All have sinned and fall short of the glory of God" (Rom. 3:23).

What is sin? Everyone talks about it, and most of us assume we know what it is, but we should pause a moment to define it before we go any further. Probably the most commonly held conception of sin is that it is wrong acts, bad deeds, or, as children come to think of it, being naughty. But that is an oversimplification. That is only one variety of sin. A more inclusive definition would be something like this: "Sin is any act, thought, or state that fails to conform to the moral and spiritual will of God." It means being less or other than what God is and what he desires us to be, and that can happen in any number of ways.

The Varieties of Sin

The extent of a particular group's vocabulary on a given subject matter is often a good indication of how much that subject concerns, interests, and involves them. Thus, for example, the Arabic language has over one hundred words for camel, because the camel plays such an important role in the life of many Arab people. The Arab has a word for every type of camel and for every stage in its life. English, however, has only two, camel and dromedary. Camels have a much less important place in the life of English-speaking people. When it comes to sin, the Hebrew and Greek languages are very rich. There are words for many different forms of sin, because there are so many different ways to miss God's standard of holiness and purity. Time and space do not permit us to discuss these words in detail, but it will be helpful to describe three main types of sin, that is, three main ways of failing to fulfil God's intention for us.

The first variety of sin is sometimes referred to as transgression. This involves breaking God's law, going beyond what is permitted, doing the forbidden. It is seen quite clearly in the very first sin in the Bible. God told Adam and Eve that they could eat of the fruit of any tree in the Garden of Eden, except one—the tree of the knowledge of good and evil. That was off limits to them. Yet that was the tree whose fruit they chose to eat. Many of God's commands are put in negative fashion, indicating a prohibited activity: "You shall not kill"; "You shall not commit adultery"; and so on. The activities mentioned in these commandments are wrong, being contrary to God's very nature; therefore, doing them is sin.

It is possible to sin, however, without doing anything. For the instructions of God are not all negative prohibitions. Many of them enjoin us to take positive actions. Failure to do so is the second variety of sin, which is just as wrong as is transgression or violation of God's rules. James wrote, "Whoever knows what is right to do and fails to do it, for him it is sin" (James 4:17). Jesus said that the first and great commandment is, "You shall love the Lord your God with all your heart, and with all your soul, and with all your mind, and with all your strength" (Mark 12:30). Failure to come up to this standard, or falling short of it, is sin. If the first type of sin can best be called sins of commission, the second should be called sins of omission. Here perhaps is where most of our sins fall. For we do not generally love the Lord our God with all our being, nor do we always love our neighbor as ourselves, which is Jesus' second commandment. It is in this area that the non-Christian who seems to be so respectable, so honorable and decent, comes up short. It is hard to believe that such a person qualifies as a sinner in the sight of God. Sin, however, is not primarily a moral matter, but a religious matter. Failure to love God or to glorify him, even to give him credit for the virtuous things one does for others, is sin.

A third group of sins has an inward dimension. Here are the attitudes or ideas that accompany our actions. Even "good actions," or actions which fulfil the law of God, are sinful if done for the wrong motive. Jesus was very harsh in his condemnation of the Pharisees, who did good deeds but did them so that others would see them and be impressed. When we begin to look at sin this way, it becomes much more inclusive than before. Many of our good deeds begin to fall under this classification.

Jesus indicated that inward thoughts and motives are

spiritually significant, just as outward actions are. The Old Testament law had condemned murder and adultery, but Jesus indicated that hatred and lust are also sins (Matt. 5:21–22, 27–28). Perhaps the only reason we abstain from a sinful act is our fear of the consequences. Though we are not transgressing or breaking God's law in the formal sense, we are sinning because our attitude or motive or intention is wrong. This means that acts that appear the same may actually be very different, and many seemingly good acts may actually be evil. Imagine, for example, two salespersons. A customer comes into the store, buys a ninety-cent item, gives the first clerk a five-dollar bill, and is about to leave, obviously thinking he has given a one-dollar bill. The clerk realizes the mistake and thinks, "I could keep the four dollars for myself, and the cash register would check out at the end of the day." But although the possibility of his being detected is slight, he reasons that his job is worth far more than the four dollars. So he says to the customer, "Sir, your change!" and returns the money to its rightful owner. The second salesperson has a similar situation with a customer, but he thinks, "This money is his; it is not right for me to keep it," and so returns the cash. Externally the two acts will appear identical to an onlooker, but they are very different from the standpoint of moral virtue. Sin is a very subtle thing, sometimes deceiving others and even the person who commits it.

The Consequences of Sin

What are the results of sin? Sin has adverse effects at three different levels. The first and most serious is one's relationship to God. We may observe this consequence quite clearly in the account of the first sin. Adam and Eve's trust in God and their positive relationship of love and obedience to him were replaced by distrust and fear. Their act of rebellion and disobedience made them enemies of God. So we see Adam and Eve attempting to hide from God. A desire to avoid God and anything that smacks of religion is often the effect of sin in one's life.

Sin has a much more devastating effect, however, on our relationship to God. For the sinner comes into a state of divine disfavor. As much as God loves all his human creatures, he is constitutionally opposed to sin. It is contrary to his very nature, so that his response is as automatic as an allergic reaction. The pictures of God's anger against sin are very vivid. More than 180 times in the Old Testament a noun that can literally mean "snorting" is used of God's reaction to sin. It is used, for example, in the description of his anger against the people of Israel for making a golden calf and engaging in idol worship. It is not that the loving God changes when we sin. It is rather that we have moved from the area of what is good and righteous, of which he approves, to the area of what is contrary to his will, of which he must disapprove.

Having actually and objectively violated God's will and commands, we are guilty before him and subject to punishment. To punish sin is not something that God simply decides to do, but an outworking of his very nature. What is this punishment? One major aspect of it is death. God said to Adam and Eve, "In the day that you eat of it [the fruit of the tree of the knowledge of good and evil] you shall die" (Gen. 2:17). Similarly, Paul says in Romans 6:23: "The wages of sin is death." It would appear that this did not mean simply physical death, for Adam and Eve did not die immediately upon sinning. The most significant aspect of death is spiritual death, which is the separation of the sinful person from God. In the case of Adam and Eve, this meant being driven from the Garden of Eden. If we do not receive the new life that Christ came to offer, spiritual death becomes permanent, that is, eternal death, an endless separation from God (Matt. 25:41–46a).

The second level at which sin has adverse effects is our relationship to other humans. Adam not only sinned against God, but sought to blame Eve: "The woman . . . she gave me fruit of the tree, and I ate" (Gen. 3:12). Unwillingness to accept responsibility for one's sin and shifting the blame to someone else are not uncommon. In fact, Adam even implicitly blamed God: "The woman whom thou gavest to be with me. . . ." In the very next chapter of Genesis we find Cain, whose offering to God was not acceptable, in effect blaming his brother Abel for the problem and killing him. Part of God's will for us, by contrast, involves love for other humans. So Jesus said that the second great command was, "You shall love your neighbor as yourself" (Mark 12:31). Failure to love one's neighbor is a frequent form of disobedience to God. Wars are just a large-scale version of this type of sin.

One of the reasons for the conflict between human beings is that sin, emphasizing our own hopes and ambitions, puts us into competition with others, who may be seeking the same things we are. Ambition and acquisitiveness put people on a collision course. And it is hard to love someone whom we are trying to beat in some form of competition.

Finally, sin has direct effects upon the sinner. Enslavement is one of these effects. In order to cover one's sin, or to avoid its consequences, one has to engage in yet other sins. Cain murdered his brother out of his jealousy and sense of inadequacy. In order to avoid admitting his sin to God, he lied (Gen. 4:9). Abraham found that the sin of misrepresenting his wife as his sister (Gen. 12:10–20) was so easy to commit that he quickly repeated it (Gen. 20). It had become a habit, an established way of acting. After committing adultery with Bathsheba, David murdered her husband, Uriah, to keep the sin secret.

Self-deception is another effect of sin upon the sinner: we deny both the fact and the results of sin. Jeremiah reminded us that the heart is very deceitful and wicked (17:9). We fail to see our own sin, even though it is like a beam in our eye, but notice the speck in our neighbor's eye (Matt. 7:3). If we do recognize our sin, we like Adam find excuses to justify it. Moreover, unwillingness to acknowledge the reality, harshness, and finality of death with respect to this earthly life is commonplace. We deceive ourselves by using positive language to refer to it (see p. 154).

The Universality of Sin

Who sins? Usually it is easier for us to recognize sin in others than in ourselves, yet the Bible makes clear that all humans are sinners. Isaiah, likening humans to sheep, said, "All we like sheep have gone astray; we have turned every one to his own way; and the LORD has laid on him the iniquity of us all" (Isa. 53:6). In the New Testament the clearest and most emphatic passage is Romans 3, where Paul's heaping up description upon description of the universal wickedness in the world culminates with verse 23: "all have sinned and fall short of the glory of God." The Bible makes it plain that there are no exceptions to the all-encompassing fact of sin.

Sin entangles not only every person, but the whole of each person. It is sometimes thought that sin is focused in one aspect of our being, such as our physical nature or perhaps our will. It is, however, apparent from Scripture that all aspects of human nature are involved: the body (Rom. 6:6); the mind (2 Cor. 4:4); the emotions (Gal. 5:24); and the will (2 Tim. 2:25–26).

The Human Predicament

But if the Bible teaches that all humans are sinners, it also teaches that, without exception, we are unable to extricate ourselves from our sin. Sin is a powerfully addictive force. Any attempt to change by reforming oneself will inevitably fail. It is as if we have fallen into a well or a deep pit. We are free to jump out, and yet we are not.

We are free to jump as high and as hard as we can, yet we lack the ability to escape. Paul's frequent references to being dead in our sins have this problem in view (Eph. 2:1–2; Col. 2:13).

There is a problem, then, with any approach that believes that humans can simply improve themselves, or that the condition of the human race and of society can be righted by merely appealing to the best in people. Early in the twentieth century there were many self-help religions around. One of the most highly developed was that of the Frenchman Emile Coué, who had a little slogan: "Every day, in every way, I'm getting better and better." I have also heard a similar thought from a Christian leader: "Good, better, best. Never let it rest, until the good is better and the better is best." Sooner or later these approaches end in frustration and disillusionment. They must inevitably fail, for there is a defect, a flaw in human nature.

A Christian theologian once compiled a list of thirty basic virtues and assigned each one to a specific day of the month. On the first day of the month he concentrated on mastering the first virtue, the second day on the second virtue, and so on. When he reached the thirtieth day, however, he checked back and found that he no longer had any mastery of the first virtue, and so also with the second, the third, and the rest. Not only are we sinners because we sin, but we sin because we are sinners.

The naturalness of sinning is an indication that there is something seriously wrong with us. This is the teaching which the church has down through the years referred to as "original sin." We do not start life with a pure and innocent or even neutral nature, but we begin with a nature already inclined toward doing the wrong. Whereas Adam and Eve began with clean and unspoiled human natures (as did Jesus as well), we do not. The Bible teaches that the sin of Adam put all of us under the sentence of death (Rom. 5:12–21). Just like a child who is born with a disease or even an addiction because of the condition of a parent, or who labors to pay off a debt incurred by a parent, so we are affected by Adam's sin; and yet it was not just Adam who sinned, for in a very real sense we were all there and involved, since Adam and Eve were the entire human race at that time.

The sinfulness inherent in human nature must not be forgotten as we face the issues of life. Any plan of church outreach or political program which assumes that people are good and unselfish, and will do the right thing if they simply are shown what that is, is destined to fail. Sin is within everyone; even within the Christian it is not completely eradicated. Sin makes us more concerned about ourselves and our own interests and ambitions than about those of others, or even of God. As a little test ask yourself whose picture you look for first in a photograph of a group of which you are a part. Sin is a very real portion of human nature.

The Question of Guilt

In the title of this chapter we asked what has become of sin. For in our day sin is not a popular subject. Even Christians shy away from the subject. We do not like to admit that we are in a state of wrong relationship with God. Other analyses are offered instead. Some suggest that what we sometimes refer to as sins are simply carryovers from the days before we evolved from our animal state. We are gradually leaving them behind. The problem is that we are ignorant of what is right. With a little more instruction, that problem will be overcome. Others give excuses for our individual behavior. Our genetic inheritance, the poor environment in which we were raised, or some similar factor is responsible for our condition, which is in no way our fault or the result of our choices. Yet the Bible attributes our woeful condition to sin. We will never succeed in overcoming sin until we recognize and acknowledge its reality.

A similar problem applies to the question of guilt. Today a great deal is said against anything that would cause people to feel guilty. In fact, guilt feelings are thought to be a major problem, hindering us from being what we should be. The father of psychoanalysis, Sigmund Freud, has been greatly influential here. To be sure, there are people who have irrational guilt feelings; they feel guilty regardless of whether they have done wrong. But what of those who have committed wrongs? The solution is not to eliminate their feelings of guilt, but to eliminate the objective fact of their guilt. As one Christian speaker put it, "What are you going to do with people who are guilty? They should feel guilt."

There have been ministries, especially evangelistic ministries, which have exploited irrational guilt feelings and in so doing have done more harm than good. The problem with feelings of guilt, it has been said, is that the wrong people have them. Some persons need counseling to deal with feelings of guilt for which there is no objective basis. In other cases, however, and especially the cases of those who have never received the new birth, the feelings of guilt cannot be taken away until the guilt itself is removed by Christ's cleansing work.

Corporate Sin

We have spoken of sin primarily in individuals. It also has a social or corporate dimension. For since society is made up of sinful individuals, sin comes to expression in the very structures of society, including the political and economic. It virtually takes on a life of its own. Communal efforts to curtail and restrain the power of sin will be necessary if we are to deal successfully with some of these corporate manifestations, even though society can ultimately be changed only through the transformation of the individuals who make it up.

Sin is a serious matter. It affects and infects each one of us within society. It brings guilt, corruption, and separation from God. None of us can overcome sin by our own effort. In the chapters which follow we shall see that God, recognizing human helplessness, has acted to cancel and remove sin.

Study Guide

Key Questions

1. How would you define "sin" for someone who knows nothing about the Bible?
2. What are the three main ways that people fail to fulfil God's intention for them?
3. In what specific ways does sin alter one's relationship with God?
4. The most serious consequence of sin is spiritual death, an endless separation from God. What are some of the other significant effects of sin?
5. "Not only are we sinners because we sin, but we sin because we are sinners." How does this doctrine of original sin influence one's assessment of humankind's inherent goodness?

Bible Investigation

Carefully read through Psalm 51. Describe David's understanding of sin: its nature, its consequences, and its remedy.

Personal Application

"Even 'good actions,' or actions which fulfil the law of God, are sinful if done for the wrong motive." The Old Testament prophets spoke this truth pointedly and repeatedly. Isaiah 1:10–17 tells us that the activity of worship can actually be sinful, even when we follow God's prescribed patterns. Have there ever been times when your worship of God has degenerated into a type of meaningless ritual which God cannot endure? According to Isaiah, when is this most likely to happen?

We may assume (wrongly!) that any attempt to worship God will be pleasing and honoring to him. What kind of accompanying activity does God say will demonstrate the sincerity of our expressions of allegiance? See Hosea 6:6 and Micah 6:8.

For Further Thought

1. Various self-help groups are designed to assist people in conquering destructive and addictive behaviors. Although the support these groups offer to hurting people can be very helpful, some of their efforts have not been totally successful. We need to understand the extent to which our own wrong choices affect our condition. "We will never succeed in overcoming sin until we recognize and acknowledge its reality." To what extent should self-help groups confront sinfulness? How should such groups deal with feelings of guilt? Are guilt feelings always inappropriate? What is God's solution for objective guilt?

2. The consequences of sin are felt not only by individuals, but also corporately by the whole society; there is a social dimension to sin. In recognition of this fact, the church has often supported charitable organizations, relief efforts, and reform movements in order to alleviate some of the suffering due to sin. It has been contended that unless evangelism plays a key role in these efforts, social-action programs will have limited success. Do you agree or disagree? Why?

Suggested Additional Readings

Campolo, Anthony. *Seven Deadly Sins.* Wheaton, Ill.: Victor, 1987.

McClanahan, John H. *Man as Sinner.* Nashville: Broadman, 1987.

Ramm, Bernard. *Offense to Reason: A Theology of Sin.* San Francisco: Harper and Row, 1985.

7

Jesus—
God and Man

We come now to an issue that lies at the very heart of our Christian faith. For the question of who and what Christ is constitutes the whole basis of Christianity. If we do not know who Christ is, we Christians are in fact followers of X, and it is essential for us to find out who this X is.

One can imagine the puzzle that the early disciples had. It was clear that Jesus was the most unusual person they had ever met. He was not quite like any other human being they had known. Yet he clearly was a human being, for he had a human body as did they, ate and suffered pain just as they did, and experienced the same human emotions they did. Who then was this remarkable person who had entered their experience?

The Deity of Jesus

There are many passages in the Bible which tell us about Jesus. Probably the clearest statement of who Jesus was and where he came from is Philippians 2:5–11. In this passage Paul makes two very important points, both of which we must be sure we understand and believe.

The first point is that Jesus was and is genuinely God.

Paul is here describing what Jesus was before ever coming to this world. He was in the "form" of God (v. 6). The Greek word Paul uses *(morphē)* signifies "that which makes something what it is." Paul is saying, then, that Jesus had all the characteristics of God.

There was another Greek word for "form" which was available to Paul. That word *(schēma)* means "a mere outward appearance, a shell, mask, or façade." It is common to speak of beauty as being only skin deep, but there is a beauty which is even less than skin deep. It is a beauty that is put on, like makeup, false eyelashes, or a toupee. It can be taken off, for it is not really part of the individual. Now there is a likeness to God which is of such nature. It is an imitation of him, a copying of him, without really possessing his qualities. Christians (and even non-Christians) can learn a sort of spiritual behavior and talk that will impress believers, including ministers. Such likeness to God can be put on and taken off, just as we might do with our Sunday clothing. This, however, is not the kind of likeness to God that Paul speaks of in Philippians 2:6. He uses the other Greek word, which means "the essence of something." Jesus is of the very same stuff, as it were, as is the Father. He is as fully God as is the Father.

We should note that Jesus never said in so many words, "I am God." Because he did not, some have thought that Jesus did not really believe himself to be God. Rather, this was an idea created by some of his earliest disciples, perhaps Paul, and then attributed back to him. Is such an interpretation justified? When we look closely at Jesus' life, we see that although he never overtly made such a claim, he certainly did things and said things which reveal that he understood himself to be God.

We observe, first, that Jesus exercised powers appropriate only to God. One of the things that made the Pharisees most angry with Jesus was that he claimed to forgive sins. The Pharisees clearly understood what this meant, for they said, "It is blasphemy! Who can forgive sins but God alone?" (Mark 2:5–7). Certainly Jesus knew that, too.

Jesus also claimed the authority of God over the Sabbath. The Sabbath had been established by God as a day of rest and service (Exod. 20:8–11). Yet Jesus healed on the Sabbath day (Luke 13:10–17) and defended the right of his disciples to gather corn then, which the Pharisees viewed as laboring on the Sabbath day (Mark 2:23–28). His justification of this activity was that "the Son of man [his favorite term for himself] is lord even of the sabbath" (v. 28). For someone to claim to be able to set aside the Sabbath day is to claim a right and a power which only God has, in other words, to claim to be God or equal with God.

Finally, Jesus claimed the power of ruling and judging, which ordinarily were associated only with God. In fact, Jesus asserted that in the last times he would exercise the authority which the Old Testament assigns to God (Matt. 25:31–46).

Beyond this exercise of divine power, we find Jesus claiming a unique relationship to the Father, a clear implication of deity. He claimed to be one with the Father (John 10:30). He also told his disciples that anyone who had seen him had seen the Father (John 14:7–9). And when he said, "Before Abraham was, I am [not 'I was']," the Jews picked up stones to throw at him (John 8:58–59). It seems clear that they regarded his statement as blasphemy, as claiming to be God, which no human has a right to do. Evidently in their minds his statement, "I am," represented a claim to be the one who identified himself to Moses as "I AM" (Exod. 3:14).

There are other indications that Jesus believed himself divine. When he was tried, Caiaphas the high priest commanded him, "Tell us if you are the Christ, the Son of God" (Matt. 26:63). If Jesus were not divine, here was a perfect opportunity for him to correct the mistaken conception regarding himself. To correct the error could have saved his life. Yet he not only did not deny the charge, but in effect confirmed it by replying, "Yes, it is as you say," and then went on to declare, "In the future you will see the Son of Man sitting at the right hand of the Mighty One and coming on the clouds of heaven" (v. 64 NIV). The response of the high priest ("He has spoken blasphemy") indicates that in his mind Jesus had definitely made a claim to divinity. This is as close to a direct statement of his own deity as we can find in Jesus' words.

There is at least one other instance where Jesus accepted the attribution of deity. Having heard the report that Jesus had risen, Thomas declared that unless he could see the nail marks and stick his finger in them, and place his hand in Jesus' side, he would not believe. When Jesus appeared to Thomas and invited him to do those very things, he responded, "My Lord and my God!" (John 20:28). Here certainly was a declaration of deity. If Thomas had been mistaken, Jesus had a perfect opportunity to correct the error, and indeed an obligation to do so. Yet he did not. His silence constituted acquiescence to Thomas's declaration.

The rest of the New Testament also supports the deity of Jesus Christ. For example, the opening chapter of the Letter to the Hebrews speaks of the Son as being the radiance of the glory of God, the exact representation of his nature (1:3). It was through him that God created the world (v. 2), and the Son upholds all things by his word of power (v. 3). In verse 8, a quotation from Psalm 45:6, the Son is addressed as God. The Son is also described as superior to angels (1:4–2:9), Moses (3:1–6), and high priests (4:14–5:10).

The prologue of the Gospel of John calls Jesus the Word. John says that the Word was in the beginning, was with God, and was God (i.e., divine in nature) (v. 1). He was the one through whom all things were made; without him nothing was made (v. 3). Here is a claim of deity, linking Jesus to God in terms of both what he was and what he did.

Earlier we noted Paul's description of Jesus in Philippians 2. The same idea is found elsewhere in Paul's writings as well, for he had a thoroughgoing belief in Jesus' deity. In Colossians 1, for example, he says that Jesus is the image of the invisible God (v. 15); he is the one in whom and through whom and for whom all things were created (v. 16); he is before all things, and in him all things hold together (v. 17); in him all the fullness of God was pleased to dwell (v. 19). This last expression is repeated in 2:9, where Paul says that in Christ the whole fullness of the Deity dwells bodily. One could hardly expect to find clearer declarations of the deity of Christ.

It is important that we observe exactly what is being said about Jesus Christ. The Bible is not teaching that Jesus is one of many gods, or that he is a secondary god created by the one true God and inferior to him. Some people who call themselves Christian hold such beliefs, but this is not what the Bible says. Nor does it say that the nature of Jesus is similar to, but not identical with, the nature of the Father. He is of the very same nature, having the very same quality and character.

In the earliest centuries of the Christian church, disputes took place regarding the person of Jesus. So a formula was worked out by the bishops and theologians, and adopted at the Council of Nicea in the year 325. This formula stated that Jesus is of the very same essence or substance *(homoousios)* as the Father. Some scholars who could not quite accept the formula suggested instead that Jesus' nature is similar to that of the Father. They used a slightly different Greek word which contained one additional letter *(homoiousios)*. That was rejected, however. The council insisted that Jesus' nature is not simply similar to, but the same as that of the Father.

Cynical commentators have ridiculed this disagreement, calling it a debate over a diphthong. This would seem to be the ultimate case of hairsplitting and narrow-mindedness. But is that really so? There are, after all, some other cases where a very small change in spelling can make a very great change in meaning. In my first pastorate, I had to do much of the secretarial work myself. The custodian's teenage daughter volunteered to type and mimeograph the church bulletin, however, and this proved to be a helpful arrangement. Then one Saturday evening she called, being quite distraught. "I've made a terrible mistake," she said. "I've transposed two letters and completely ruined tomorrow's bulletin." Puzzled, I said, "Joyce, I'm sure it will be all right. The transposition of two letters can't be too serious." "Oh yes it is!" she replied. "Do you remember the announcement, 'Congratulations to Mr. and Mrs. Smith, who were united in marriage'? Well, it reads 'untied.'" There is a huge difference between being united in marriage and being untied. Similarly, there is an immense difference between being the same in nature as and being similar in nature to the Father.

It is important to realize that the divine nature of Jesus is unique among human beings. If our understanding of human nature is correct, we will understand this point. There are some persons, however, who believe that each of us humans has a bit of the divine, a spark of deity, within; Jesus simply has more of it than we do. One of the most serious charges lodged against a theologian of the Church of Scotland who was tried for heresy in the late nineteenth century was that he denied the divinity of Jesus. Hurt and feeling unjustly treated, he complained, "How can they say that? I've never denied the divinity of any man, especially not Jesus!" That is not what we mean by the divinity of Jesus. We mean that he is fully God in the same way and to the same degree as is the Father, and in a way that no other human has ever been or ever will be.

The Humanity of Jesus

The deity of Jesus is crucial to Christianity. The other point which Paul makes in Philippians 2 may seem quite obvious, but is equally important to maintain: Jesus was

DOES IT MATTER WHAT I BELIEVE?

fully human. Paul tells us in verse 7 that Jesus took the very nature of a servant and was found in appearance as a man. There are numerous other places in the New Testament that witness to the full humanity of Jesus.

The beginning of Jesus' earthly life was both supernatural and natural. His mother Mary was a virgin who had conceived through the supernatural agency of the Holy Spirit. Yet the birth itself was just like that of any other infant. And after describing the birth Luke tells us that Jesus developed just as do other human children: he grew "in wisdom and in stature, and in favor with God and man" (Luke 2:52). He went through the processes of maturation that are part of human life.

Subsequent descriptions of Jesus' life show the various signs of humanity. For example, he felt hunger when he had not eaten (Matt. 4:2). The hunger pangs which he underwent were as genuine as those you and I feel in a similar situation. He felt and gave expression to thirst, as seen especially on the cross (John 19:28). He was fatigued by labor and lack of rest (John 4:6). He was capable of suffering physical death, and did (John 19:33). People were able to see him, hear him, and even touch him (1 John 1:1).

It is important to understand the extent of Jesus' humanity. He took upon himself the whole of human nature, all parts of human nature. Some people think that the incarnation of Jesus means that he took a human body, that he was human physically. To take on human nature fully, however, means to take all of the psychological dimensions of human nature as well. In addition to a human body, he had a human mind and personality. Not only did he grow in stature (physically), but, according to Luke, he also grew in wisdom (intellectually), in favor with man (socially), and in favor with God (spiritually).

The biblical picture of Jesus reveals typical human emotions and psychological experiences. He loved, as humans love one another: John is spoken of as the disciple "whom

Jesus loved" (John 13:23). He felt and showed compassion for the hungry, the ill, the grieving, the lost (Matt. 9:36; 14:14; 20:34; Mark 1:41; 6:34; 8:2; Luke 7:13). The Greek verb in these verses very vividly indicates the emotion which Jesus displayed. We speak of feeling emotion with the heart, but the Greeks pictured the emotions as located in the visceral organs; thus the word for "feeling compassion" is derived from a word for the visceral organs. Jesus also felt joy (John 15:11; 17:13; Heb. 12:2).

We have mentioned what we usually think of as positive human emotions. Jesus also felt the emotions that we sometimes label less positively. Thus he felt anger and indignation, a legitimate and appropriate emotion in certain situations (Mark 3:5; 10:14). He was astonished at the faith of one (Luke 7:9) and at the unbelief of others (Mark 6:6). At Lazarus's tomb he was "deeply moved in spirit and troubled" (John 11:33), and wept (v. 35), and was "deeply moved again" (v. 38). The verb here is used of horses' snorting. So deep was Jesus' emotion that he sighed audibly. He was troubled in Gethsemane (Matt. 26:37–38; cf. John 12:27) and on the cross (Mark 15:34), where he also felt loneliness.

Jesus had a human mind as well. By choosing to become incarnate in human form, he accepted certain limitations, even upon his knowledge. He asked a father, for example, how long his son had suffered from a certain condition (Mark 9:21). There are, to be sure, situations in which we ask a question to which we already know the answer. Teachers do this type of thing all the time. In this particular situation there is little reason to believe that this is what Jesus was doing. There is, on the other hand, every reason to believe that he asked because he genuinely did not know. A major area regarding which Jesus acknowledged ignorance was the future, especially the time of his second coming (Mark 13:32). However, it is important that we distinguish between ignorance and error. Jesus did not know certain things, but he realized that he did not know, so he did not speak out on matters of which he was inadequately or inaccurately informed.

There is one other point which we should make. This pertains to what we might call Jesus' religious life. He attended worship at the synagogue regularly (Luke 4:16). He prayed to the heavenly Father. In every major crisis of his life, we see him praying; before choosing his disciples, for instance, he prayed all night (Luke 6:12). Even though he was God, he found it necessary to renew himself spiritually by praying to the heavenly Father.

The Mystery

Yes, Jesus was fully God and fully human. Like the Trinity, this is one of the mysteries of the Christian faith. We wonder how one person could be both God and man, for he was not two persons functioning together within the shell of a single human body. Nor was he some hybrid that was really neither deity nor human. He was both in one person. That is difficult to conceive of, for God is unlimited in certain qualities in which humans are limited. How could Jesus be both?

A few thoughts will help somewhat to alleviate the puzzle, although they will not solve or remove it completely. We must realize that what God did in the incarnation was to voluntarily restrict the exercise of his divine powers: the Second Person of the Trinity (Christ) could exercise them only in dependence upon the First Person (the Father). In a sense, this is akin to what God does when he makes a promise or a covenant with human beings. He is free either to do or not to do a particular thing, but once he pledges himself to do it, he is no longer free not to do it. Similarly, in the incarnation Christ was still fully divine, but his deity was exercised in connection with the humanity which he had chosen to assume.

One analogy that has helped me is a three-legged race. In each team of two, the right leg of one partner is tied to the left leg of the other. Now one of the partners may be the fastest runner in the world. His physical capability is not diminished during the race; the muscles of his leg do not shrivel. But he can exercise his running ability only in connection with his partner. Even if the partner is the second fastest runner in the world, they can't run as fast together as can the third fastest runner by himself. Similarly, in the incarnation God the Son chose to exercise his omnipresence only in conjunction with the physical body of Jesus of Nazareth.

All of this is an amazing truth. God the Son was willing to leave the comfort and glory which were his to come to this earth and take on the conditions of humanity. That is real love. In the next chapter we will see how much it cost him.

Study Guide

Key Questions

1. What two basic truths concerning Jesus are found in Philippians 2:5–11?
2. What are the implications of Jesus' being the very "form" of God? See also Colossians 1:15–22; 2:8–10. How should one respond to Jesus' deity?
3. To what extent did having a human body subject Jesus to the type of experiences and physical limitations that we have?
4. How can an appreciation for the humanity of Jesus help one to pray confidently? See Hebrews 4:14–16.

Bible Investigation

"Jesus never said in so many words, 'I am God.'" Read the following passages, each from a different Gospel, to draw some conclusions concerning who Jesus understood himself to be: Mark 2:1–12; Luke 6:1–5; John 10:24–39; Matthew 25:31–46.

Personal Application

According to opinion polls, an overwhelming majority of Americans believe in the existence of God, and yet it's probably safe to say that most of them have no ongoing personal relationship with him. To what extent is an understanding of who Jesus is necessary to know God? See John 14:1–11.

Many people who reject Jesus actually know very little about him. With such people in view, try describing the person of Jesus Christ in one concise paragraph.

For Further Thought

Certain cult groups acknowledge the significance of Jesus Christ but deny his deity. If you were confronted with the proposition that Jesus was indeed the Son of God without actually being God, how would you respond? Consider John 1:1–18; 10:24–39; 20:24–29; 1 John 5:20.

Suggested Additional Readings

Bruce, F. F. *Jesus: Lord and Savior.* Downers Grove, Ill.: Inter-Varsity, 1986.

McDonald, H. D. *Jesus—Human and Divine: An Introduction to New Testament Christology.* Washington, D.C.: University Press of America, 1989.

McGrath, Alister E. *Understanding Jesus: Who Jesus Christ Is and Why He Matters.* Grand Rapids: Zondervan, 1987.

Walvoord, John F. *Jesus Christ Our Lord.* Chicago: Moody, 1974.

Prophet and Priest and King

When we think of the work of Christ, we are given an added measure of understanding and are filled with a sense of wonder as well. Here it is that the facts about Christ which we investigated in the previous chapter begin to make sense. Now we can understand why he came as he did. But there also is an increased sense of wonder and awe, for we are even more conscious of the greatness of his grace in the incarnation.

At the mention of Christ's work our thoughts almost immediately go to his death, and that is natural, for his death is his most significant work and has the most far-reaching consequences. It is, however, not the only ministry of Christ. Christians have occasionally thought about Christ's work in terms of three roles which he performed, or three offices which he filled: prophet, priest, and king. In the Old Testament these roles were separated and filled by different persons. To help us understand better what Christ has done for us, we will look briefly at each of these offices.

Prophet

Jesus performed supremely the role of prophet. He followed in the tradition of the Old Testament prophets, who came bringing a message from God for his people. Jesus' ministry went beyond that of the Old Testament prophets, however, for he did not simply have a message; he was the message! He did not merely receive a word from God and then tell others; rather, he himself came from the very presence ("bosom") of God (John 1:18). Beyond the Old Testament prophets' function of declaration, Jesus had the function of exhibiting. He was God, and so his very life and actions set forth what God is like. He could say, "He who has seen me has seen the Father" (John 14:9). And unlike the prophets, who called their hearers to believe with them in the one whom they proclaimed, he called upon his hearers to believe in him.

Priest

Jesus made his major contribution in his role as priest, a special office which he alone could fill. The Old Testament priests had offered sacrifices to God on behalf of the people. These sacrifices, as important as they were, had only a temporary effect. They could cover past sins, but could neither prevent nor cover future sins. Thus, with additional sin, additional sacrifice had to be offered. Jesus' sacrifice, by contrast, was of eternal value.

To understand the death of Christ and what it accomplished, we have to go back and refresh our thinking a bit about the nature of sin. Sin, you will recall, carries with it the consequence of guilt or liability to punishment. This is a penalty which God must impose because sin is an offense against his very nature and against the fabric of the moral system which he has established. And you will recall that one dimension of this penalty is death, physical, spiritual, and eternal: "The wages of sin is death" (Rom. 6:23). This is a penalty which must be paid.

We have nothing with which to pay the penalty but our own lives. Thus, for a balance to be restored in the moral and spiritual system of the universe God rules over, each person would have to suffer everlasting death as punishment for sin. Yet this penalty need not be borne by the individual who is personally guilty of the sin. Just as in a court of law, where someone else can pay a fine for a guilty party, so Christ can put himself in our place and suffer the consequences of our sin. This he did on the cross.

There are several reasons why it was possible and appropriate for Christ to pay the penalty for us. His death is of value to the human race, because he was one of us; he was genuinely human himself. Further, his death is of sufficient value to cover all the sins of all humans who have ever lived, because he is God. His life was of infinite value. Beyond that, he could die for our sins because he did not have to die for his own. Had he been a sinner like the rest of us, he would have had to bear the consequence of death just to atone for his own sins. But since he did not have to die, his death could go beyond himself and serve to achieve our salvation, the forgiveness and remission of our sins.

That Christ bore our punishment is made clear in many places. In fact, one of the Greek prepositions used of his dying "for" us (anti) means, literally, "instead of" or "in place of." Just as the sacrificial animal in the Old Testament was offered in place of the sinner, so Christ stepped into our spot. His death was the sacrifice which spared us from the consequence of our sins, namely, death.

There are other aspects to and purposes for the death of Christ, although our salvation is primary. For instance, his death serves to show how serious sin is, and how far God will go to redeem us. If sin is serious enough for God to put his own Son to death, then it must certainly be no trifling matter. We must not regard sin lightly, as if it were something that God can ignore by simply looking the other way.

The death of Christ together with its aftermath is also a powerful demonstration of the defeat of the powers of evil. We know from the Gospels that the religious leaders of the times were intensely opposed to Jesus. As agents of the forces of evil, they sought desperately to get him out of the way. They thought they had found the perfect means, namely, to put him to death. Then he would no longer be able to teach and perform miracles. This was Satan's ultimate weapon. Yet it could not defeat Jesus. On the third day, about thirty-six hours after his death and burial, Jesus was alive again. Even death, which had come into the world through sin, could not control him. Think of how the news of the empty tomb must have struck those who had put Jesus to death. Even that had failed! What more could they do? There would be no point in killing him again; even if that could have been done, he presumably would have simply come back to life again. We might think of the death of Jesus in terms of Satan's taking the bait and then being caught in the trap. The death of Jesus symbolizes and foreshadows the complete destruction of the forces of evil.

It is important that we keep this aspect of the death of Christ in mind. In a world in which evil seems so powerful, in which Satan fights so desperately, there sometimes is a tendency for us to despair, to wonder if we can do anything. Jesus, however, has already struck the crucial blow in the fight. In places like Africa, where the forces of evil are so active, this aspect of Christ's atoning work can be especially encouraging.

Another purpose of the atoning work of Christ was to demonstrate the greatness of God's love for us. The amazing thing about this love is that there is in us no real basis for it. It is not as if God found us naturally lovable or even likable. It was while we were yet sinners, while we were still in rebellion, rejecting God's love for us, that he sent his Son to die for us. This is true love indeed.

In addition, the death of Christ is the most complete example of the attitudes and behaviors God expects of us. Christ's obeying the Father even to the point of giving up his life is the type of devotion that God desires from us. In a sense, Jesus' serving as an example is more a function of his prophetic role than of his priestly role, for it makes known to us what God wants us to know.

In dying, Christ paid the penalty for us, defeated evil, demonstrated infinite love, and served as an example. We are reminded of the ancient story of the blind men and the elephant. Each one took hold of a different part of the animal and then shared his general impression. The man who seized one of the legs thought the elephant was like a tree, the man who grasped the tail thought the elephant was like a rope, and so on. All were right, but had only a part of the truth. In like manner, each of the several theories of the atonement, as they are sometimes called, expresses a different aspect of the truth. The atonement is such an important and profound truth that it is like a multifaceted diamond. We need to examine each of the facets individually and yet keep them all together. At the same time we must be aware that the most basic truth, the one without which the others would not exist, is that Christ took our place to pay the penalty for our sin.

Sometimes the death of Christ is pictured as a great injustice. How can it be that someone who himself was innocent of any wrongdoing, who in fact was the only completely innocent person ever to live on the earth, was punished in our stead? Is this not immoral? Suppose a jury found a defendant guilty, and then the judge condemned an innocent third party to serve the sentence. Is this not what the Father did to the Son?

Two observations need to be made. First, the decision to die for us was voluntary on Christ's part. He said, "I lay down my life" (see John 10:15–18). This was not something forced upon an unwilling victim. Second, although the Son bore the direct effects of our sin, the Father was not an uninvolved bystander. Just as parents today suffer when their child suffers, and sometimes a more excruciating pain, so the Father suffered, too. Father and Son were one, and both participated, as did the Holy Spirit, in the decision that Christ should come and die;

and all experienced, in varying fashion, the pain of the suffering.

If we have fully understood the doctrine of the atonement, it will have a profound effect upon us. It will make us truly grateful for all our Lord has done for us. Without his death, we would be lost in our sins and would have to suffer endless death for them. So whenever we speak or sing of the Lord's death for us, and whenever we partake of the Lord's Supper, we will be deeply moved. Although the Lord's Supper is a celebration of the victory over evil, it can never be a time of lighthearted frivolity, for that victory was purchased for us at a very great cost. While living in a monastery, Martin Luther was once found kneeling before a crucifix and, with tears streaming down his cheeks, repeating over and over, "For me, for me, for me!" The biblical understanding of the Lord's death stresses the fact that he did it for us.

There is one other aspect of the priestly work of Jesus Christ. One task of the Old Testament priest was to intercede with God in behalf of the sinner. This Christ does supremely. He has not left us without resources. Not only does the Holy Spirit live within believers, but Christ himself intercedes for us. He fully understands what we go through and the sorrows and temptations we bear, because he himself was completely human. The writer of the Letter to the Hebrews says, "For we do not have a high priest who is unable to sympathize with our weaknesses, but we have one who has been tempted in every way, just as we are—yet was without sin" (Heb. 4:15 NIV). We sometimes forget that his humanity was such that he could and did experience what we do, and thus he can understand.

Sometimes this truth comes home to us with surprising force. Several years ago I was writing a major book. It was a project which took many months to complete. During this period I would rise early and work late every day, keeping myself to a severe schedule to try to finish within the time allotment which I had. I frequently experienced fatigue and weariness. I came to my work without excitement, even though I knew God had called me to it. I remember one January day in particular. I really did not want to write that day. I felt discouragement, realizing how much of the project was still ahead of me. My topic that day was the humanity of Jesus. I soon came upon Matthew 26:37–38, which says that Jesus was sorrowful and troubled. I thought, "That's just what I am feeling, and Jesus felt it too! He understands what I am going through today, because he went through similar circumstances." That was a most uplifting experience. Buoyed by the thought that Jesus was there with me and saying, "I know what you are feeling. Come on, I know you can do it!" I did more than the usual amount of work and felt very good at the end of the day. The humanity of Jesus means that he is able to help us. He can understand and answer our prayers appropriately because he has experienced all of the burdens that we do.

King

Jesus is also the king of all of creation. His reign is real; although it is incomplete and partly invisible at the present, one day it will be complete and fully visible. During the time of Jesus' earthly ministry, his kingship was not always evident. To be sure, the wind and the waves obeyed him, reminding us that he is the Lord over all of nature. The demons were subject to his command, reminding us that he is the Lord of the spiritual realm. And at least some of the humans whom he encountered acknowledged him as Lord and accepted his leadership.

One incident which illustrates the complex truth that Christ's reign will someday be fully visible is his triumphant entry into Jerusalem on what we now call Palm Sunday. Within the very week in which the people would reject him as Savior and Lord and crucify him, God provided them with a glimpse of the future that is to be. For a moment, the kingly Christ was seen. The owner of the donkey on which Jesus intended to ride provided the animal without hesitation. And the animal, an unbroken colt, without protest allowed Jesus to ride. The disciples and the crowd cried out their praise to Jesus. They waved their palm branches and laid their garments down in his path. When the Pharisees told Jesus to restrain his followers, he replied, "If these were silent, the very stones would cry out" (Luke 19:40). Jesus is truly the king of all that is, a fact which was richly manifested on that day.

Everything that exists obeys (or someday will obey) its Lord in ways that are appropriate to its nature. The inanimate creation obeys Christ mechanically. The planets, stars, and other heavenly bodies move in their courses because they follow the natural laws that Christ structured into the universe. So precise is this obedience that we can pinpoint the movements and locations of these bodies over a period of centuries. Without any conscious awareness of what they are doing, these servants of Christ carry out his commands.

Animals also obey the patterns that they have been given, but they do so instinctively. Salmon returning to spawn in the exact place where they were hatched, and the swallows returning annually on March 19 to San Juan Capistrano, are obeying the patterns embedded within them. Although presumably conscious of the impulses that move them, they do not choose either to follow or not to follow them.

It is only human beings that can choose to serve Jesus as their king and Lord. Their obedience is all the more glorifying to him because it is unforced. For we have been made by God in his own image, which includes the power to reason and think, emotions, and freedom of choice. Ironically, some use this God-given endowment to rebel and reject him. Those, however, who make Christ their Lord and the leader of their life, are fulfilling what they were intended by God to be, and bring the greater glory to God as a result.

We have said that, sooner or later, everyone will serve Christ the king. Some have within this lifetime chosen to make him their Lord; they have voluntarily become subject to his reign. But when he comes in the last days as victorious king and judge, all will be subject to him. Paul says that "at the name of Jesus every knee [shall] bow, in heaven and on earth and under the earth, and every tongue confess that Jesus Christ is Lord, to the glory of God the Father" (Phil. 2:10–11). Many in that group will be submitting involuntarily as vanquished, defeated subjects. For them, the kingdom of Christ will not bring joy, but anguish and regret at not having become subject to him earlier.

There is debate over whether Christ's rule is present or future. In the fullest sense his reign lies in the future; it is yet to be. He is like a king who has the right to a territory, but is not actively exercising that right because he has not yet been crowned. But Christ's reign is also present, for his kingdom exists wherever there is obedience to him. Each of us can help to make his reign an increasing reality, a highly desirable goal, for his reign is characterized by peace and righteousness, and restores the world to what it was originally intended to be. We can help achieve this goal by living in accordance with his Word. We will follow his commands not as frightened slaves who fear the consequences of disobeying, but as friends who desire to please him (John 15:14). This is not legalism. Rather, this is the way we show our love for our Lord, who said, "Whoever has my commands and obeys them, he is the one who loves me" (John 14:21 NIV). We can also spread Christ's kingly rule by telling others of him, so that they too may come to obey and serve him. And finally, we can help to bring about his reign by working for the kind of righteousness that he desires, by endeavoring to have his will done in this world. For in the Lord's Prayer the petitions "Thy kingdom come" and "Thy will be done, on earth as it is in heaven" (Matt. 6:10) have virtually the same meaning.

Sometimes we focus our thinking almost exclusively on what Christ did during his earthly ministry. What he did then was surely of crucial importance, for it made possible our new life and our eternal future with him. But he has not been inactive since his departure from earth. At the ascension he resumed the position he had with the Father before coming to earth. He is now seated at the right hand of the Father, and is ruling over the earth from there. He is now encouraging, helping, accompanying, and interceding for us. And one day he will come again to make his reign complete.

What Jesus has done, is currently doing, and is yet to do is a grand and glorious, sometimes overwhelming thought. It is small wonder that the hymnwriter burst forth with these words:

> And can it be that I should gain
> An interest in the Saviour's blood?
> Died he for me, who caused his pain?
> For me, who him to death pursued?
> Amazing love! How can it be
> That thou, my God, shouldst die for me?
>
> (Charles Wesley, 1738)

Study Guide

Key Questions

1. How would you briefly describe the three offices of Jesus that help clarify for us the reasons why he came to earth?
2. What is meant by the atoning death of Christ? What was its primary purpose?
3. Besides sparing us from the consequences of sin, Christ's death accomplished several other purposes. What are they?
4. What priestly function does Jesus perform for believers on a daily basis?
5. In what three ways can each of us help to make the reign of Christ an increasing reality?

Bible Investigation

Read Hebrews 1:1–3. What evidence do you find in these verses that Jesus filled the roles of prophet, priest, and king? In what ways is Jesus superior to earthly prophets, priests, and kings? See Hebrews 1:8–9; 7:23–28; 9:11–15; 10:11–18.

Personal Application

"What Jesus has done, is currently doing, and is yet to do is a grand and glorious, sometimes overwhelming thought." Certainly such a thought should provoke a response. Read Hebrews 10:19–39. How should someone who really understands and appreciates the ministry of Christ respond to it?

For Further Thought

Today we accept Jesus as our king. He is both the king of all creation and the ruler of our hearts. At the time of Jesus' ministry on earth, the Jews were anticipating the coming of a king, one who had been promised to them by the prophets of long ago. Compare the prophecy of

Zechariah 9:9–17 with the question asked by the apostles in Acts 1:6. What kind of king did the Jews expect? How might what happened at Jesus' triumphal entry into Jerusalem have supported their view? See Mark 11:10. What is the nature of the kingdom that Jesus preached? Is it more of a realm or a reign? Consider Matthew 4:17; 6:33; Luke 11:20 (note the context); Acts 1:3; Romans 14:17; Revelation 1:5–6.

Suggested Additional Readings

Dominy, Bert. *God's Work of Salvation.* Nashville: Broadman, 1986.

Morris, Leon. *The Atonement.* Downers Grove, Ill.: InterVarsity, 1984.

———. *The Cross of Jesus.* Grand Rapids: Eerdmans, 1988.

Sanders, J. Oswald. *The Incomparable Christ: The Person and Work of Jesus Christ.* Rev. ed. Chicago: Moody, 1982.

9

The Least-Known Member of the Trinity

The Holy Spirit is at once one of the most important and yet one of the most misunderstood topics of Christian belief. This is a strange and unfortunate situation which requires some careful examination. Let us begin by looking at why a correct understanding of the person and work of the Holy Spirit is important.

First, the Holy Spirit is the member of the Trinity through whom the Godhead becomes personal to us. The Father is transcendent, removed in heaven. The Son's life upon earth is historically removed, two thousand years in the past. But the Holy Spirit lives within us and works with us in special ways. He is the one who gives us new birth and sanctifies us, making us holy.

Second, the Holy Spirit plays an especially prominent role in the world today. Just as the Father is highlighted in the Old Testament and the Son in the Gospels, so the Holy Spirit is the most prominent member of the Trinity in the Acts and the Epistles, and he has continued to be so through the present time.

Third, this is a day in which personal experience is

emphasized in many areas of our culture. It is the Holy Spirit through whom we especially experience God and feel him at work in us.

The Reasons for the Confusion

There are reasons why many Christians today are confused and even ignorant about the Holy Spirit. The first is that the Bible says less about the Holy Spirit than about the Father and the Son. A large part of the Spirit's ministry is to declare and glorify the Son (John 16:13–15). Among the few extended treatments of the Holy Spirit are John 14–16 and Romans 8.

Further, there is a lack of concrete imagery to help us in our thinking about the Holy Spirit. When we talk about God the Father, we form a mental picture of a father, and we go through a similar process with respect to God the Son. But the Holy Spirit? We can't come up with an analogy from our own experience. In addition, some of us who have used the King James Version of the Bible, which refers to the Holy Ghost ("ghost" meant "spirit" in seventeenth-century English), may find that the image that comes to mind is something in a white sheet.

The role played by the Holy Spirit in the present age may lead us into confusion also, if we do not understand clearly the biblical witness regarding him. Just as the Son subordinated his role to that of the Father during the time of earthly ministry, so the Holy Spirit subordinates his role to the Father and the Son during the present period of God's working. Consequently, just as some Christians incorrectly conclude that the Son is actually lower than the Father, so some may infer that the Holy Spirit is less than the Father and the Son. This, however, is an incorrect deduction as well. It is easy to fall unconsciously into the error of thinking of the Trinity as FATHER, SON, and holy spirit. But they are all equal in nature; all are equally God.

Sometimes Christians have been hesitant to engage in

study and discussion of the Holy Spirit, because that topic has frequently led to controversy. I know of one pastor who refers to "the Holy Spirit problem" in his church. Having had to deal with a divisive controversy about the gifts of the Holy Spirit early in my first pastorate, I sympathize with that pastor, but the Holy Spirit is not the problem. The problem is that a better understanding of the Holy Spirit is needed. It simply will not do to avoid the topic, for it will surely come up when we least expect it and the circumstances are less than ideal.

The Person of the Holy Spirit

It will be wise to consider who the Holy Spirit is before we go on to what he does. Note that I said "who" he is rather than "what" he is. For the first thing to observe and understand about the Holy Spirit is that he is a person. He is not a force, a power, or anything of that type. He is a person, with all of the capabilities for relationships and interaction which that entails. He has will, intellect, and emotions. He wills what gifts shall be given to whom (1 Cor. 12:11). He can be lied to (Acts 5:3), grieved (Eph. 4:30), and resisted (Acts 7:51).

The Holy Spirit is fully God as well. Certain Scripture passages speak of God and the Holy Spirit interchangeably. Peter speaks of Ananias and Sapphira's sin as both lying against the Holy Spirit (Acts 5:3) and lying to God (v. 4). In 1 Corinthians 3:16–17 Paul tells his readers that their bodies are the temples of God and that the Holy Spirit dwells within them, and then in 6:19–20 he tells them that their bodies are the temple of the Holy Spirit and that they should glorify God in their bodies. The Holy Spirit is also mentioned in such close connection with the Father and the Son that we have to conclude that he is fully their equal; among the texts in view here are Matthew 28:19; 1 Corinthians 12:4–6; 2 Corinthians 13:14; and 1 Peter 1:2.

The Work of the Holy Spirit

When we come to the study of what the Holy Spirit does and has done, we find a rich variety of activities. It is sometimes difficult to identify the Holy Spirit in the Old Testament, since the term usually used there is "Spirit of God." This is not surprising, since the Hebrew language uses adjectives much less than does English; Hebrew prefers, for example, an expression like "man of holiness" to "holy man." Yet it is apparent that "Spirit of God" and "Holy Spirit" are synonymous. For it is clear from Acts 2:14–21 that Peter regarded the events of verses 1–11, which fulfilled Jesus' promise of the coming of the Holy Spirit (Acts 1:8), as also fulfilling Joel's prophecy regarding the outpouring of the Spirit of God (Joel 2:28).

In the Old Testament we find that the Holy Spirit was involved in the original work of creation and continues to be active in the universe (Gen. 1:2; Job 26:13; Isa. 32:15). He gave craftsmen the various skills necessary to construct the tabernacle (Exod. 31:3–5). He gave powers of administration (Num. 11:25; Deut. 34:9). In the Book of Judges these powers seem especially related to the ability to wage war successfully (Judg. 3:10; 6:34; 14:19).

Our knowledge of God is in large part a result of the work of the Holy Spirit. It is he who inspired writers to record God's revelation, so that we now have the Bible. Again and again prophets testify that the Spirit of the Lord came upon them (Ezek. 2:2; 11:1, 5, 24). Peter tells us that the Holy Spirit spoke by the mouth of David (Acts 1:16; 4:25), and that the prophets, being moved by the Holy Spirit, spoke from God (2 Pet. 1:21). The Spirit also gives the believer understanding of the Bible, an activity which we call illumination (John 14:26; 16:13–14).

The Holy Spirit is at work in the various stages of the Christian life. It is apparent that he plays a vital role at its beginning. This is the work of conviction; the Spirit convinces us that we are sinners and that provision has been made for the overcoming of our sin. Jesus promised that the Spirit would do this (John 16:7–11). But the major change that takes place when there are repentance and faith is the regeneration or the "new birth" of the individual (John 3:3). Jesus explained this as being "born of the Spirit" (vv. 5–8). It is the Spirit who effects this wondrous change in us, which no amount of human effort or reformation can accomplish.

At the point of regeneration each believer is baptized by the Holy Spirit into the church universal. (This should not be confused with water baptism, which inaugurates us into a local church or body of believers.) Since Pentecost each believer has had the Holy Spirit dwelling within. Jesus told his disciples that the Spirit was with them and would be in them following his own departure from the earth (John 14:16–17). That promise was repeated at Jesus' ascension (Acts 1:8) and fulfilled at Pentecost (Acts 2). Now the Holy Spirit dwells within us, making us and our bodies his temple. Whereas in the Old Testament the Holy Spirit came dramatically upon believers for a definite purpose and for a limited time, he now dwells permanently within.

The indwelling of the Spirit means that he has access to us in ways that even Jesus during his earthly ministry did not have to his disciples. Jesus was himself led and empowered by the Holy Spirit (Matt. 12:28; Mark 1:12; Luke 4:14, 18–21). He said that his followers would do even greater works than he had done (John 14:12), for his going away would enable the Holy Spirit to come to them (John 16:7). That the Holy Spirit is able to affect from within how we feel, think, and make decisions is a source of great encouragement and comfort to believers.

As the *Holy* Spirit, he is at work seeking to produce holiness in the believer. The technical term for this activity is sanctification. Paul makes much of this work of the Spirit, which he contrasts with the life of the flesh. The Spirit guides and witnesses to the believer (Rom. 8:1–17).

He creates a set of qualities which are collectively referred to as the fruit of the Spirit: love, joy, peace, patience, kindness, goodness, faithfulness, gentleness, self-control (Gal. 5:22–23). These qualities cannot as a group be produced by human concentration and effort, which result only in works of the flesh (vv. 19–21).

It is important to understand that the Holy Spirit's guidance is tied to the lordship of Christ and the content of what God has revealed to us in the Bible. Jesus said that the Holy Spirit would "bring to your remembrance all that I have said to you" (John 14:26). We are not to look for new revelations of truth or doctrine. What the Spirit does is to give us understanding of what has been supplied in the Bible, and to apply that truth to specific situations. Thus he may, through my studying the Bible, visiting another country, or hearing the message of a missionary, create the conviction that he wants me to become a missionary. This may even, through the opening of a door of opportunity, be as specific as a particular country, for example, Japan. That guidance, however, is only for me. He will not give me some new message for all believers, as that all Christians should become missionaries to Japan. Nor will he give me a revelation of some new truth that is not found at least implicitly within the Bible, as that there is a fourth divine person in the Trinity (which should therefore be renamed Quadrinity). Furthermore, his specific leading will never be contradictory to the truth of Scripture. He will never, for example, tell me that I should murder someone.

Understanding the nature of the Spirit's guidance is important, for strange, unwise, and even unholy things have sometimes been done in his name. Some people think they have a special direct connection with God, when what they actually have are strongly held opinions. The Spirit who inspired men to write the Scriptures does not give messages contradictory to his own Word.

The Results of the Spirit's Work

It is worth noticing the results of the Holy Spirit's work in the individual as well as in the church. One of the first things that we observe is power. Jesus said, "You shall receive power when the Holy Spirit has come upon you" (Acts 1:18). The sermon which Peter preached at Pentecost was not remarkable from the standpoint of technical quality, although we have no way to judge the nonverbal dimensions of Peter's delivery. Probably many preachers today could prepare and deliver a better sermon. It is, however, difficult to criticize the results, for three thousand persons were converted. One pastor has said, "Peter preached one sermon and had three thousand conversions. We preach three thousand sermons and are lucky to have one conversion." The conversions at Pentecost were not the result of Peter's sermonic ability or oratorical skill, but the work of the Holy Spirit.

The Holy Spirit also produces unity in the church. The early believers were "of one heart and soul" (Acts 4:32). They did not even consider their personal property as being their own. They sold what they had and put the proceeds into a common treasury for the benefit of anyone who had need. The Holy Spirit produced a unity which could even be felt, for when the believers prayed, the place in which they were gathered was shaken (v. 31). The Holy Spirit binds people together in harmony. While there may be times when it is God's will for individual believers to separate from others who identify themselves as Christians, we can be certain that the Holy Spirit is not at work where there is disharmony.

Further, the Holy Spirit thrusts people outward to witness. Jesus said, "But you shall receive power when the Holy Spirit has come upon you; and you shall be my witnesses" (Acts 1:8). Obeying Christ's commission, the church went forth in the power given by the Holy Spirit and took the Good News into the world. Thus it was that the Lord added to their number daily those who were being saved (Acts 2:47).

We must again remind ourselves that the Holy Spirit produces the fruit of the Spirit. One of the best tests of whether the Spirit is at work in us is the extent to which we embody those qualities. They will accompany his working. He does not work through bitterness, pride (in the sense of boastful arrogance), or lust. The Spirit-controlled believer will clearly manifest love, joy, and peace.

The Gifts of the Spirit

One of the most significant and yet controversial issues for Christians is the gifts of the Spirit. It is important to recognize the breadth of this topic, for the gifts conferred by the Spirit are many. There are no fewer than four different lists: Romans 12:6–8; 1 Corinthians 12:4–11; Ephesians 4:11; and 1 Peter 4:11. Included in these lists are various types of servants whom the Spirit gives to the church, such as pastors, evangelists, and apostles. There also are spiritual qualities, such as faith and service, which all believers are expected to have and practice, but which apparently some are enabled to exercise in an extraordinary fashion. Finally, there are some unusual supernatural powers, such as healing, the working of miracles, and speaking in tongues. It is important to understand that all of these gifts are granted to the church for the edification, the building up, of the body (1 Cor. 12:7; 14:5, 12).

While all of the gifts of the Spirit are special, some are more attractive and thus seemingly more desirable than others (1 Cor. 12:22–24). No one person has all of these gifts (vv. 14–21), nor is any one gift possessed by everyone (vv. 29–30). This is why we need each other, and why there is diversity within the body. It is the Holy Spirit who sovereignly determines who receives which gift (v. 11). There is no indication that any gift is conferred upon someone on the basis of being more worthy than others.

It is with respect to the more spectacular or supernatural gifts that dispute is sometimes found within churches today. There are some who claim to have and exercise these gifts, especially the gift of speaking in tongues. Sometimes they intimate that this is a mark of a special level of spirituality (the baptism of the Spirit or the second work of grace). They may claim that speaking in tongues is a gift that all believers are to have and ought to seek. It is regarded as giving special power. Since it was present in the New Testament church, it should be present in our New Testament Christianity today.

Opposed to this position are those who say that the gift of tongues and the others like it have ceased. They were intended for the period of the establishment of the church and the completion of the biblical revelation, but they are not found today and should not be sought. Speaking in unknown words and any similar episodes that occur today are understood as psychological phenomena or the results of satanic working. Parallels in pagan religions are pointed out.

Given these two polar extremes, it is not hard to see why controversy and conflict occur. We do not have sufficient data to prove either that the spectacular gifts of the Spirit ceased with the end of the New Testament period, or that they are still being bestowed today. In a practical sense, it may not matter, for we are not told to seek any specific gift. In fact, after urging his readers to earnestly desire the higher gifts (1 Cor. 12:31), Paul immediately calls them to the practice of love (ch. 13), terming this the "more excellent way" (12:31). It is important to remember that no gift is for all believers, and that the Holy Spirit in his sovereignty decides who will receive which gift. The emphasis is upon the spiritual quality of love rather than the exercise of any one gift.

We should note that Paul commands his readers not to forbid speaking in tongues (1 Cor. 14:39). What are we to do, then, if someone claims to have this gift and proceeds to exercise it in a public gathering of believers? Here

Paul has laid down certain guidelines, which it would be well to follow: only one person should speak in tongues at a time, there should be no more than two or three speakers, and an interpreter should be present (1 Cor. 14:27). If no interpreter is present, the would-be speaker should remain silent. As always, the building up of the body, not the satisfaction of the individual, is paramount (vv. 12–19).

A Proper Response to the Holy Spirit

The doctrine of the Holy Spirit is a precious doctrine, for the person and the work of the Spirit are precious. If we understand him correctly, certain actions will follow:

1. We will honor the Holy Spirit as God, just as we do the Father and the Son. It is appropriate to worship him and to direct prayer to him.

2. We will claim the promise that he intercedes for us when we do not know how to pray (Rom. 8:26–27).

3. We will give the Holy Spirit control over our lives. This we will do by asking him to guide and sanctify us, and by turning ourselves, including our thoughts, feelings, and wills, over to him.

4. We will ask the Holy Spirit to illumine our minds, to give us understanding and conviction of the truth of the Bible which he has inspired, and to apply it to our lives.

5. We will exercise the gifts that the Holy Spirit has granted us for the building up of the body of Christ, the church; we will also seek fellowship with other believers, so that the gifts that the Spirit has given them may build us up as well.

Study Guide

Key Questions

1. What scriptural evidence can you give that the Holy Spirit has equal status with God?
2. How was the Holy Spirit active in the Old Testament?
3. What is the Holy Spirit's role in salvation?
4. What was the main work of the Holy Spirit at Pentecost? See Acts 1:8.
5. What are the differences between the fruits of the Spirit and the gifts of the Spirit? How is each group distributed?
6. What are the two most widely held viewpoints regarding the baptism of the Spirit?
7. What does a filling with the Holy Spirit empower one to do? See Acts 4:31.
8. In 1 Corinthians 12:31 what does Paul mean by the "higher gifts"?

Bible Investigation

Certain eras in church history and certain religious traditions have focused their attention on a specific member of the Trinity, often to the neglect of at least one of the others. Contrary to this practice, it is important to tie our theology of the Trinity to Scripture. Carefully consider John 16:13–15 and Colossians 1:15–29. What do you discover from these passages about the role of the Holy Spirit? What insights do you get concerning the relationship of the Spirit to the Son? Where should our attention be directed?

Personal Application

1. How exactly does the Holy Spirit illumine Scripture for a believer? Would the use of commentaries and other study aids help or hinder this work of the Holy Spirit?

2. How does the Holy Spirit guide a person in decision making? Does making careful plans run contrary to listening to the Holy Spirit? What exactly is being condemned in James 4:13–16—planning for the future or a disregard for God's sovereignty? How can one distinguish between a leading of the Holy Spirit and a strong personal desire or mere wishful thinking?
3. How does the Holy Spirit produce unity in the church? Can unity be achieved when church leaders have differing temperaments? when there is disagreement on styles of worship and music?

For Further Thought

Ephesians 5:18 contains a command to Christians to "be filled with the Spirit." This implies that Christians have control over whether or not they are filled! Can a believer be filled with the Spirit more than once? Does this mean that we need to seek more of the Spirit? to offer more of ourselves to his control?

Suggested Additional Readings

Biederwolf, William E. *Study of the Holy Spirit.* Grand Rapids: Kregel, 1985.

Davis, Earl C. *Life in the Spirit.* Nashville: Broadman, 1986.

Inch, Morris A. *The Saga of the Spirit.* Grand Rapids: Baker, 1985.

Ward, Wayne E. *The Holy Spirit.* Nashville: Broadman, 1987.

10

So Great Salvation

Salvation is truly an amazing aspect of the Christian's life. For it is what makes us new creatures and children of God. It is what guarantees us that we will go to heaven. It is so unusual that Jesus spoke about it as being "born again."

Conversion

To understand what salvation is, we first have to understand what the human problem is, or what we have to be saved from. We saw in chapter 6 that all human beings are sinners living apart from God and in rebellion against him. We sin because we cannot avoid doing so. We are sinners in our very makeup. Salvation from that tragic condition is something God does for us, but in order to receive it, we have to make a complete about-face, because sin means that we are going in diametrically the wrong direction. This change of direction is called conversion. The Greek word that is translated "conversion" means, literally, "a turning." In Acts 9:35, for example, Luke tells of a mass conversion when "all the residents of Lydda and Sharon . . . turned to the Lord."

Conversion has two aspects. It is both a turning from

sin and a turning to Jesus Christ. The turning from sin is called repentance. True repentance is a godly sorrow for sin, simply because sin is wrong and an offense to God, rather than because it leads to unfortunate consequences for us. The need to repent was preached by John the Baptist (Matt. 3:2), by Jesus (Matt. 4:17), by Peter (Acts 2:38), and by Paul (Acts 17:30). Repentance is not easy, it is painful. Someone has said that the most difficult words in the English language to pronounce are, "I was wrong," and the next most difficult words are, "I am sorry." They are painful. And repentance is especially painful because it involves admitting that we have done wrong morally and spiritually and are truly sorry for it. Yet unless we repent and are willing to give up sin, we are not really converted.

The other side of conversion is faith. Faith involves believing certain facts to be true, whether about God (Heb. 11:6) or Jesus (Matt. 16:16–19; Rom. 10:9–10; 1 John 4:2; 5:5). If we do not correctly identify him to whom we are turning, this side of conversion will be empty of content. But mere acceptance of doctrines alone is not enough for salvation. James tells us that even the demons believe that God is one—and shudder (2:19). Faith also involves personal trust. It is a matter of acting upon what we believe, and asking Christ to save us, while also declaring that we want to make him the Lord of our lives.

This combination of repentance and faith makes up conversion, the turning from the old ways of sin and toward Christ. Although it is essential that there be such a conversion, the specific circumstances may vary greatly from one person to another. For some persons conversion takes place at a single, easily identified point in time. It may even happen the very first time one hears the message of Christ. For others conversion may involve a prolonged process of gradually coming to repentance and faith. They may not be able to point to a specific moment and say, "That's when it happened!" But turns can be sharp or gradual, whether on roads or in life. In central Wisconsin there is a place where two major highways meet. An eastbound driver who wants to go north must first turn south. The road then forms a large semicircle approximately one-half mile in circumference, so that one makes a 180-degree turn. The change of direction is so gradual that one cannot point to a given spot and say, "Here's where I started driving north!" There also are times in life when one makes a gradual U-turn. Whether our conversion is gradual or rapid, the most important thing is that we are now able to affirm that we are heading in the right direction.

There is one other respect in which conversions vary. For some people, especially those who have sudden conversions, there is a very vivid emotional experience which includes tears of sorrow and then of joy. For others, especially those whose conversion is gradual, there is little or almost no emotion. Stories of the former, especially if they involve a person who has lived in gross and heinous sin, are more dramatic than stories of the latter. We sometimes tend to elevate emotional conversions as a model, and consequently persons who have had quieter conversions may wonder about the genuineness of their salvation. Here it is important to remember that one's basic personality type, circumstances in life, and many other factors affect the nature of the experience. Within one chapter (Acts 16) Luke tells the dramatic conversion story of the Philippian jailor, but also the quiet story of Lydia, of whom we read that "the Lord opened her heart to give heed to what was said by Paul" (v. 14). It is not how we felt when we changed directions, but, rather, the direction in which we are now heading, that makes the difference.

Union with Christ

We have spoken of the richness of salvation, which like a jewel has many different facets which should be examined. Is there one underlying conception which gathers up all of the facets, one key to the whole of salvation? I believe the one concept that covers and explains all of what God does in response to our repentance and faith is union with Christ. We are united with him in a bond like a marriage or a legal corporation.

The Bible speaks much of our union with Christ. Paul speaks of the believer as being in Christ: "Therefore, if any one is in Christ, he is a new creation" (2 Cor. 5:17). Conversely, he wrote, "Christ [is] in you, the hope of glory" (Col. 1:27), and "It is no longer I who live, but Christ who lives in me" (Gal. 2:20). And he wrote frequently of the believer's being "with Christ": we have been crucified with Christ (Gal. 2:20); we have died (Col. 2:20), been buried (Rom. 6:4), been made alive (Eph. 2:5), and raised with him (Col. 3:1); we are joint heirs with Christ, provided we suffer with him in order to be glorified with him (Rom. 8:17). Union with Christ certainly appears to be the key factor in understanding our relationship to him and to salvation.

Justification

What precisely does union with Christ mean? It means, first, that we are merged with him, judicially and legally. When a man and a woman marry, their financial assets are merged. The debts of each one become the debts of both, and the assets of each one become the assets of both. If one partner has a debt of $10,000 and the other has a bank balance of $15,000 and owes nothing, together they are solvent, with a net worth of $5,000. A similar situation holds with respect to our spiritual condition.

We observed earlier that sin puts us in debt to God; we are liable to punishment and have nothing with which to pay. The only thing we can do, therefore, is to die eternally. There is a popular theory that the way to be saved is to live a good life; if we heap up enough good deeds, we will become acceptable to God. The problem is that we never can acquire a positive balance. Every good thing we do has already been required of us, since God said we are to be perfect as he is perfect. Consequently, we can do nothing to compensate for our inevitable failures. The only way in which the problem can be solved is by a merger with Christ. Not only did he fulfil the requirements of God's law completely, but he, the one person of whom death was not required, since he never sinned, died in my place. Therefore, if I have accepted Christ, when God looks at me, he does not see me alone, but he sees me with Christ. All of my sin and all of Christ's righteousness are merged; united with him, I am now just or acceptable to God.

Justification is not quite what we sometimes think it to be. God does not merely pretend that I have the righteousness of Jesus. He does not look at me and say, "We will not count his sin, but rather Christ's goodness." No such stratagem is necessary, for through my union with Christ his righteousness has actually become mine!

Nor is justification quite what the little slogan says, "Just as if I had never sinned." It is true that my guilt, my liability, is now no greater than it would be if I had never sinned, but there is a difference between, on the one hand, never having sinned and, on the other, having sinned and paid the penalty (or, in this case, having had the penalty paid on my behalf). There has been a learning experience, an experience of forgiveness. Beyond that there is profound gratitude for having been given the righteousness I could never have attained by my own effort.

Justification is much richer than mere forgiveness in the sense of cancelation of a debt or penalty. When criminals have served their sentence, they are released from prison. Their debt to society has been paid. That does not mean that society welcomes them back with open arms, however. Unfortunately, there may be discrimination, distrust, or, at the very least, a polite coolness. By contrast, justification involves adoption: God the Father welcomes us into his family and shows the love that a devoted father gives to his child. We are not just pardoned criminals, but sons and daughters of God (John 1:12; Gal. 4:4–5; Eph. 1:5).

Regeneration

Becoming one with Christ entails more than just having his righteousness, however. Righteousness is merely the formal state of being free from the penalty of sin. Union with Christ also entails holiness, the positive condition of being good, of actually becoming what the law now considers us to be. We come to be like Christ himself, to show his love, mercy, faithfulness, and all his other positive qualities. Attaining Christlikeness is a process that has a beginning (regeneration), a continuation (sanctification), and a completion (glorification).

Jesus spoke to Nicodemus of being "born again." This is a reference to the beginning of the Christian life. Paul wrote of how the unbeliever is dead in trespasses and sins (Eph. 2:1, 5; Col. 2:13). Like a part of the body that has been anesthetized and can feel nothing, so the unbeliever is insensitive to spiritual concerns. If there is to be life, it must come from outside. There must be a new beginning. In addition to Jesus' statement to Nicodemus, the New Testament contains several other passages that use various terms to refer to new birth or regeneration: John 1:12–13; 2 Corinthians 5:17; Ephesians 2:1–2, 5–6; Titus 3:5; James 1:18; 1 Peter 1:3, 23; 1 John 2:29; 5:1, 4. More-general statements are found in John 6:63 and 10:10, 28; and a parabolic form appears in Luke 15:24, 32. There even seems to be an Old Testament reference to the new birth (Ezek. 11:19–21).

New birth occurs when we become united with Christ. Like an artificial heart connected to our circulatory system, Christ supplies the spiritual vitality that we do not have and could not acquire by ourselves. A new impetus, a new strength, is given. We come alive to spiritual things. While the creation of new spiritual vitality is the particular work of the Holy Spirit, our union with Christ is its basis.

Jesus said that he had come to give life (John 10:10), and likened the relationship between believers and himself to that between branches and a vine (John 15:1–7). Just as the branches derive their vitality from the vine, so our spiritual life comes to us from Christ. It is not something that we can achieve ourselves by reform or resolve. It is something done supernaturally in and to us, a transformation of life.

Sanctification

The new birth is just the beginning. Sometimes Christians become disappointed or discouraged because they still fall so far short of what they think they should be and what they think God expects them to be. It is important to remember, however, that the new birth is just that, a birth, and birth is merely the beginning of life. Much more growth and development must take place. Sanctification, being made actually holy or good, is the continuation of what was begun in new birth. It also is a result of our being united with Christ. Sanctification is what Paul was referring to when he wrote to the Philippians: "For I am confident of this very thing, that He who began a good work in you will perfect it until the day of Christ Jesus" (1:6 NASB).

As with conversion, sanctification in a sense has both a negative and a positive aspect. The negative aspect is the progressive removal of the old nature—the sinful tendencies, attitudes, and ways of thinking that carry over from before the new birth. Paul speaks of putting the old nature and its lusts to death. This process may sometimes involve suffering; like the surgeon, God occasionally finds it necessary to inflict pain. Not that God is cruel, but that he wants strength and wholeness to emerge. Peter wrote of this (1 Pet. 1:6–7) as did James (1:2–4).

Sanctification is not just the removal of the old sinful life without replacing it, however. That would be like trying to remove the air from a bottle by pumping it out. It is much simpler to remove the air by displacing it with something else, such as water. Some Christians try to achieve the Christian life simply by avoiding certain practices, but that is both painful and grotesque. It also is impossible. Here is where the positive aspect of sanctification comes into play. Living through us, Christ produces the fruit of the Spirit in place of the works of the flesh.

The fruit of the Spirit is not something we gain through our own effort. It is God's work in our lives. This is not, however, a process in which we can allow ourselves to be passive, waiting for him to produce the fruit in our lives. Paul, speaking of this work of sanctification, wrote, "Continue to work out your salvation with fear and trembling, for it is God who works in you to will and to act according to his good purpose" (Phil. 2:12–13 NIV). The English word *energize* is a transliteration of the Greek verb Paul uses for God's work in the believer. Paul did not see what we do and what God does as separate from one another, for we have been united with Christ, and the Holy Spirit dwells within us.

Do we ever within this life reach a state of perfect sanctification, where there is no sin in our lives? Before you answer that question, think back upon what sin is. You will remember that it is not simply wrong deeds; it is also wrong attitudes and thoughts, for example, anger or lust. It is failure to do what God expects of us. It is doing the right thing out of a selfish motive. It is failure to be as pure and holy and righteous and loving as God himself is. With this broad conception of sin in view, fine, godly Christians differ on whether perfection is possible on earth. There is basic agreement that we ought always to set our goals high in the Christian life, to seek by God's grace to continue to grow. One group maintains that we can arrive at a state of sinless perfection. God would not have commanded us to be perfect, if it were not possible. If with his help we can resist any individual temptation that comes our way (1 Cor. 10:13), then we should also be able to avoid every one of them. The other group points out that even such a giant of the faith as Paul never claimed to have attained perfection (Phil. 3:12). Clearly, then, complete freedom from sin awaits the future time of freedom from temptation.

It should be noted that the word *perfect* does not mean "flawless" or "free from any imperfection." Rather, it means "complete." Further, the fact that one does not arrive at total conformity to God's will does not mean that this is not to be our goal. Indeed, many godly believers testify that the closer they come to Jesus Christ in their personal spiritual growth, the more sensitive they become to sin, and the more upset by matters in their own lives that they previously had not considered to be sin.

Perseverance

One question that plagues some believers is, "Could I ever lose my salvation?" They notice the warnings against apostasy in the Book of Hebrews, and worry that they might fall into such a state. They may also have known persons who seemed to be committed Christians, but who at some point turned from their faith and now do not make any claim to be believers. Is there any assurance for them?

There are, of course, verses in the Bible which speak of our persevering to the end, or of Christ's keeping us to the end. But does that mean that once saved we may do anything? Can we live any way we wish without losing salvation? Does not such a view lead to a rather shallow and indifferent Christian life? If so, "once saved, always saved," must be a dangerous doctrine.

This is not an easy question to solve. In John 10:28 Jesus said, "I give [my sheep] eternal life, and they shall never perish." Actually, what he said was stronger than that. The Greek reads more like, "I give them eternal life, and they shall not, I repeat, shall not, ever perish at all."

John uses here one of the strongest forms in the Greek language, the double negative, which was a perfectly proper construction when one wanted to make a point very emphatically. On the other hand, Hebrews 6:4–6 says, "It is impossible for those who have once been enlightened, . . . if they fall away, to be brought back to repentance" (NIV).

How can these two statements both be true? It is important to note that they are not speaking to exactly the same issue. The writer to the Hebrews is discussing a hypothetical situation; namely, what would be the case if one were to turn away from the faith. (Incidentally, it is worth noting that no matter how we interpret the passage, it precludes the teaching that one can be a Christian, lose salvation, *and regain it.*) Jesus, however, is telling us what *will* happen, namely, his sheep will not perish. The Bible then can be understood as saying that we *could* fall away, but through the keeping power of Christ we *will* not. But what of the warnings against falling away? They are one of the means God uses to keep us in his grace. In one of the ways parents keep a child from being hit by a car, God keeps us from losing salvation. He does not build a fence that we cannot get out of no matter what we do, but he gives us instructions and warnings, so training us that we will not wander into danger.

There is no basis here for presumption or indifference. If we use the slogan, "Once saved, always saved," we need to be sure to put the emphasis on *once saved* rather than on *always saved.* One theologian who most forcefully taught the doctrine of eternal security was asked, "What do you say about the Christian who claims, 'I'm saved, so now I can live as I please'?" The theologian responded, "Of one thing you can be sure: that person is not a Christian. Real Christians don't think that way." People who once appeared to be Christians and then fell away were not real Christians in the first place. Appearances can be deceiving; even one of Jesus' closest followers apparently was a thief all along and eventually betrayed him (John 12:6). So the doctrine of perseverance should encourage us to trust God for his keeping rather than become presumptuous about how we may live.

Glorification

Finally, there is the great doctrine of glorification, which we sometimes overlook. The Bible teaches that the process of sanctification will be completed in connection with the second coming of Christ. Our growth in godliness will then be complete (Phil. 1:6; Col. 1:22). There will also be the final vindication of the believer, as the deeds of all are made public (Matt. 25:31–46; Luke 13:22–30). We will have complete knowledge and a perfect vision of Christ (1 Cor. 13:9–12; 1 John 3:2). Our struggle with temptation and sin will be over. That salvation which Peter said is reserved in heaven for us will be fully ours (1 Pet. 1:4–5).

This is a glorious set of truths. And it is a glorious experience to have God at work developing in us that likeness to him for which we were created, and to know that one day his work will be complete. So then, the Christian can sing with joy:

> Dear Savior! when before thy bar
> All tribes and tongues assembled are,
> Among thy chosen will I be,
> At thy right hand, complete in thee.
> Yea, justified! O blessed thought!
> And sanctified! Salvation wrought!
> Thy blood hath pardon bought for me,
> And glorified, I too shall be!
>
> (Aaron R. Wolfe and
> James M. Gray)

Study Guide

Key Questions

1. To what does the term *conversion* refer?
2. What is the nature of true repentance? What is necessary besides regret over one's sins?
3. Why is "belief that certain facts are true" not an adequate definition of "faith"?
4. All born-again individuals should be able to identify a point in time when they were converted—do you agree or disagree? Why?
5. What are the implications of being united with Christ?
6. Why is the phrase "just as if I had never sinned" inadequate as a description of justification?
7. How is the Holy Spirit linked to the process of regeneration?
8. How is the work of sanctification accomplished?

Bible Investigation

In describing how we come to be saved, many Christians cite Ephesians 2:8–9: "For by grace you have been saved through faith; and this is not your own doing, it is the gift of God—not because of works, lest any man should boast." Does this passage imply that salvation is not related to works? Are knowing and assenting to the truth of the gospel enough? What is the nature of saving faith? How are faith and works related in James 2:14–26? What is it that reveals the greatness of the faith of the individuals who are listed in Hebrews 11? How would you explain to an inquirer what is implied by the word *believe* in John 3:16 and Acts 16:31?

Personal Application

God in his sovereignty has chosen to depend upon willing human servants to spread his gospel of salvation to the world. In fact, every Christian has been commissioned and empowered to do this work. Does this empowering eliminate the need to prepare oneself for the task? (See 1 Pet. 3:15. Those who cite Matt. 10:19–20 as evidence that one doesn't need to prepare should note the context. A special provision is being made for those who will have to speak under severe persecution and need the Spirit's assurance.)

If *today* you were presented with the opportunity to share the gospel of salvation, how would you proceed? Where would you begin? Many tracts are available to help one present the gospel message. Secure several different examples from a Christian bookstore and make a comparison of their contents. Which aspects of salvation are stressed? Which are missing or not stressed enough?

For Further Thought

Sometimes there is such a strong focus on "the hour I first believed" that the richness of some of the other facets of salvation has not always been fully appreciated. Scripture presents salvation as being much more than that act by which we escape hell and gain eternity. We have already seen that sanctification and glorification are other aspects of the salvation process. Should we then regard a Christian's salvation as a past act, a present process, or a future blessing? See (1) John 5:24; 10:9; Ephesians 2:8; (2) 1 Thessalonians 4:3–7; 5:23; Hebrews 12:14; 13:20–21; (3) Philippians 3:20–21; 1 Peter 1:3–5; 1 John 3:2.

Suggested Additional Readings

Hull, William E. *The Christian Experience of Salvation.* Nashville: Broadman, 1987.

Kevan, Ernest F. *Salvation.* Philadelphia: Presbyterian and Reformed, 1973.

Ryrie, Charles C. *So Great Salvation.* Wheaton, Ill.: Victor, 1989.

Toon, Peter. *Born Again.* Grand Rapids: Baker, 1987.

11

Christianity in the Collective Form

The new life of the Christian that we examined in the preceding chapter is not a solitary life. While salvation comes to us as individuals, our new life is not restricted to that level. God intends each believer to be part of a collection of believers, known as the church.

All of us know something about the church, or at least we think we do. If you were to stop people on the street and ask them what the church is, you would probably get widely differing answers. Some would identify the church with a building, others with a denomination, such as the Lutheran church or the Presbyterian church. Still others would think of it as all of Christianity, as in the phrase "separation of church and state."

We need to make an immediate distinction between the universal church and the local church. The universal church is the entire body of believers, the regenerate followers of Christ from all times, including both those on earth and those in heaven. The local church is a group of believers who gather in one place for the purpose of combined ministry.

The New Testament word for "church" *(ekklēsia)* is actually a word for the gathering of the citizens of a Greek city or town. It is also used in the Greek translation of the Old Testament to denote the assembly of Israel. Literally, the term refers to those who are "called out" into a meeting of some type. It is not uncommon to hear a sermon in which this literal meaning is cited as evidence for the separation of the church from the world. Certainly the idea of separation from the world is taught in the Bible, but it cannot be found in this word, which pictures nothing more than a "calling out" of people from their houses into some type of assembly.

Images of the Church

While the New Testament utilizes many different images to depict the church, three in particular stand out as clear expressions of its nature. Each of them brings to mind one of the members of the Trinity: the people of God, the body of Christ, and the temple of the Holy Spirit.

The concept of the people of God ties together the Old Testament people (Israel) with the New Testament people (the church). New Testament texts which develop this idea include 2 Corinthians 6:16; 1 Thessalonians 1:4; and 2 Thessalonians 2:13–14. In the Old Testament, the sign of the covenant which made Israel God's people was circumcision. In the New Testament, this was replaced by inward circumcision, circumcision of the heart (Rom. 2:29; Phil. 3:3). So now the people of God includes all whom he has called, Gentile as well as Jew (Rom. 9:24). The emphasis of this image is that we belong to God and should therefore strive to emulate his holiness.

The second image, the body of Christ, emphasizes the present activity of Christ through both the universal church and the local congregation. Among the places where this image appears are 1 Corinthians 12:12–31; Ephesians 1:22–23; and Colossians 1:18. Among its various implications are Christ's headship over us, the interconnectedness of each believer with every other, and the need for Christ's ministry to continue through us.

The image of the church as the temple of the Holy

Spirit completes this triune picture (1 Cor. 3:16–17; 6:19; Eph. 2:21–22; 1 Pet. 2:5). The emphasis of this image is upon the Spirit as the giver of power (Acts 1:8). He creates unity, although not necessarily uniformity (Acts 4:32). He reminds believers of the Lord's teachings (John 14:26). He decides who shall receive which spiritual gift and then confers it. Because Jesus speaks of the church only twice (Matt. 16:18; 18:17), and because Luke never uses the word in his Gospel but about twenty times in the Book of Acts, the belief that the church began with the coming of the Spirit at Pentecost seems reasonable.

The Purpose of the Church

In a very real sense, the church is the continuation of Christ's ministry in the world. As his body, empowered by his Spirit, it is to do greater works than he did (John 14:12). It is to engage in activities which carry out his mission. The first of these is worship. Worship, the adoration and exaltation of God, is a recurrent theme and basic purpose of the Book of Psalms. Similarly, the pictures of heaven in the Book of Revelation represent the people of God as recognizing and declaring the greatness of God. Moreover, the author of Hebrews cautions his readers not to forsake assembling together (Heb. 10:25). It is therefore appropriate that believers under the new covenant gather together to worship their God.

A second purpose of the church is edification—building up and encouraging one another. This, according to 1 Corinthians 12:7; 14:4–5; and Ephesians 4:12, is the reason for the gifts of the Spirit. Edification is accomplished through several means: instruction and education; fellowship and sharing, whether of burdens or of joys; preaching and exhortation.

Evangelism is a prominent part of the church's task. Jesus instructed the church to go and make disciples (Matt. 28:19), and promised that the power to do so would be supplied when the Holy Spirit came (Acts 1:8). The Book of Acts is the chronicle of the church's obedience to the Lord's command. This outreach was to encompass all people from all nations, near and far.

Finally, the church is to engage in social ministry. Far from separating social concern from the more "spiritual" pursuits of the church, Jesus tied it very closely to the very nature of the body of Christ. In his prophecy regarding the great final judgment, he seems to make ministry to those in need the major criterion separating the sheep from the goats (Matt. 25:31–46). His parable of the good Samaritan clarifies the meaning of loving one's neighbor (Luke 10:25–37). James speaks against those who show favor to the rich (2:1–9), and urges care for widows and orphans (1:27). And John, in his First Epistle, urges love that is not only in word, but also in deed (2:15–17; 3:17–18). Although each church may have its own way of dealing with the evil in society, some sort of ministry of compassion is necessary to continue the work of him who healed the sick and cast out demons.

Worship, edification, evangelism, social ministry—all are important functions within the church. Sometimes they become mixed together, to the detriment of one or the other. Frequently in evangelical churches it is worship that is slighted. A worship service becomes so geared to evangelism that real worship is squeezed out. At other times a congregation may have just begun to worship genuinely when there comes the exhortation to "stand up, turn around, and shake hands with your neighbors." Fellowship has intruded into worship. We must bear in mind that each one of these activities is essential. Nothing must be allowed to interfere with its taking its due place in the life of the church.

The Organization and Government of the Church

A major question regarding the church is the nature of its organization. This is frequently the difference that separates one denomination from another. In general, there are three major types of church organization or church government: the episcopal, the presbyterian, and the congregational. There also are some church fellowships which virtually eliminate any kind of organization; they rely instead upon an inward speaking by the Holy Spirit to the members of the group. An example is the Society of Friends, also known as Quakers.

The episcopal type of government places authority in a particular office, the bishop. This form of government is found in the Methodist church, in the Anglican or Episcopal church, and most fully in the Roman Catholic Church. The bishop has the power to ordain and to appoint ministers to churches. Some groups, such as the Anglicans and the Catholics, have more than one level of bishop, with archbishops placed above the ordinary bishops; the Catholic church of course has its supreme pontiff, the bishop of Rome, the pope.

The presbyterian system of government is practiced by the Presbyterian and various Reformed churches. It places church authority not in an office, but in a series of governing or legislative bodies. While episcopal government is dictatorial or aristocratic in form, presbyterian government is more of a representative democracy. The members of the local church choose elders to represent them in the session, which is the governing body of the local church. The session in turn chooses representatives to the presbytery, which governs the affairs of a group of churches in a given geographical area. The presbytery chooses representatives to the synod, which covers a larger area, and to the general assembly, which governs the entire denomination.

The third form of government, the congregational, is practiced by the Congregational, Baptist, and many Lutheran churches. This strives to be a pure democracy in practice. Each local congregation is independent. Its members own the church property and choose and call their minister. The congregation may unite with other churches in associations or conventions to carry out their common tasks more effectively, but such affiliations are purely voluntary. Within the local church each member has one vote, and all major decisions are made by a democratic vote in an official meeting of the members of the congregation. Whereas episcopal government has several levels of clergy, including pastors and bishops, and presbyterian government has elders, both ruling and teaching, congregational government has only one lay office, that of deacon, and one level of clergy, the pastor. While some positions may carry a more specific designation, such as trustee, treasurer, or usher on the one hand, and minister of pastoral care or of Christian education on the other, these are simply subsidiary offices or variations of the basic two.

There is a twofold difficulty in deciding what type of governmental organization to adopt. On the one hand, the pattern in the New Testament church itself is not unequivocally clear. Beyond that, the extent to which the New Testament pattern was intended to be normative for all times and situations is nowhere spelled out. Each form of government has certain strengths and certain drawbacks. What we must do is to look for biblical principles which can be utilized to construct an appropriate contemporary form of church government.

One basic principle certainly is the value and even necessity of order in the church. This was seen most clearly in Corinth, where confusion and disruption prompted Paul to write to the church that "everything should be done in a fitting and orderly way" (1 Cor. 14:40 NIV). One method of achieving order is to assign certain persons to specific ministries. In Jerusalem, for example, seven men were appointed to minister to the widows (Acts 6).

Another principle is the priesthood of all believers. Since Jesus continues to serve as the sole mediator between God and us, and since the Holy Spirit dwells in every Christian, we are able to approach God directly and be led by him. This is taught by several texts (Rom. 5:1–5; 1 Tim. 2:5; Heb. 4:14–16). A third principle is that each person is important to the whole body. This truth is implicit in many places in the New Testament and is explicitly expounded in Romans 12 and 1 Corinthians 12. Each person is important, for each one's gift is necessary to the edification of the whole. Accordingly, decision making should be broadly based, and, indeed, group consensus was important in the Book of Acts (Acts 4:32; 15:22).

When all of these considerations are taken into account, it appears to me that the congregational form of church government best fulfils the biblical principles. It takes seriously the priesthood of believers. As a matter of practical functioning, however, it may be wise and necessary for the group to delegate some of its authority to an individual or a committee. Moreover, it is important to remember that the priesthood of all believers does not mean that we are all entitled to our own opinion. The individual's opinion or conviction must always be made secondary to the good of the whole. Only after careful and extended prayer and reflection should one's privilege as a member of the body be exercised. Democracy, after all, is a far different thing from anarchy. An additional consideration here is that the church is not a simple democracy, but a democracy under God, that is, a theocracy.

The Special Practices of the Church

There is a great deal of variation among those groups which call themselves churches. Nonetheless, there are certain practices in which all of them engage. Two practices found in virtually all Christian churches are baptism and the Lord's Supper. Some churches call these practices sacraments, suggesting that they convey some spiritual benefit. Others refer to them as ordinances, calling attention to the fact that our Lord is the one who ordained them and commanded their continued observance. While they may be called by different names, and be administered and interpreted differently, all churches agree that they are of great significance.

Baptism is in most churches' teaching linked in some way to the beginning of the Christian life and one's relationship to the church. It was preached by John the Baptist, commanded by Jesus (who himself submitted to it), and proclaimed by the early church. Sacramentally oriented churches, such as the Roman Catholic and Lutheran, see baptism as the means by which the person is regenerated and thus enters the church universal. Reformed groups see it as a sign of the covenant: like circumcision under the old covenant, baptism serves as evidence that we like our parents belong to the new-covenant community. Baptists generally understand the act of baptism as an expression of faith and public identification with the Lord; essential for membership in the local church, it proclaims the new birth which has brought one into the universal church. The first two groups baptize infants, the third will baptize only those who have come to a conscious and responsible faith of their own.

Different modes of baptism are practiced: pouring, sprinkling, and dipping (immersion). Immersion was used in the early centuries even by what is today the Roman Catholic Church; it is virtually the universal mode practiced on the mission field. Because it most closely embodies the literal meaning of the Greek word for "baptism" (which has been transliterated, not translated, into English), and best symbolizes our death, burial, and resurrection with Christ (Rom. 6:1–11), I find it to be the best means of fulfilling Christ's command to baptize (Matt. 28:19–20).

The other major rite (if we may term it that) of virtually all churches is the Lord's Supper. It is observed at various intervals—from daily to weekly to monthly to quarterly. All agree that it is a commemoration of Christ's death, and so has a special spiritual value, not unlike an enacted sermon. Sacramentally oriented churches believe that grace is conveyed to the recipient of the elements. Some of them, taking the words of Jesus ("This is my body. . . . This is my blood," Matt. 26:26–28; Mark 14:22–24; Luke 22:19–20; 1 Cor. 11:24–25) very literally, hold that the bread and wine (or juice) actually become the body and blood of Christ. Others regard his words as a metaphor, like the many others that he employed. In all of these views, the Lord's Supper calls to mind not only Christ's past work on the cross (1 Cor. 11:24–25), but also our present relationship with the Lord (vv. 27–32) and with other believers within the body (vv. 17–22), and the future coming of Christ (v. 26b). It is thus an integral part of Christian practice.

The Invisible Church and the Visible Church

We spoke earlier of the distinction between the universal church and the local church. These are sometimes also termed the invisible and visible church. We need to come back to that distinction again. The universal church is pure in the sense that it is made up only of believers. There is also a unity within it, for it has one Lord and head. These qualities are not always present within the local churches. We should therefore be concerned that the visible church be made as much like the invisible church as possible.

Ideally, the local church should consist entirely of true believers, born-again Christians. In practice, that will probably not be the case. We ought not to be totally surprised, since even one of Jesus' twelve was apparently not a genuine follower of him, and Jesus spoke in one of his parables of the weeds which grow among the true grain. Yet, because it is not always easy to distinguish the true from the false, care should be taken in any effort to remove the impurities. The church is not a collection of persons who are perfect spiritually. It is a group of growing believers, not of perfect specimens, and all of us have to walk by the grace of God, seeking his forgiveness and restoration frequently, as even Peter and the other disciples had to.

The Unity of the Church

Jesus prayed that his followers might be one, as he and the Father were one (John 17:22). We, too, should make it our goal that the church on earth, the saints here living for and serving the Lord, have that sort of oneness. But what is the nature of that oneness? It certainly is a spiritual oneness, since we all have the same Lord. It should show itself in such agreement of mind and such willingness to share with one another and work together as characterized the early church. The first believers were so detached from self-seeking that they did not consider their personal property to be their own, but to belong to others. Real unity today, whether or not it takes that precise form, will require the same sort of self-forgetfulness. Unity will also involve love and concern for those Christian groups who, though their understanding on relatively minor matters may differ from ours, hold the basic tenets of the faith. We must work together with them wherever the ministry can be strengthened by cooperative endeavor.

Must there be some sort of organic unity beyond cooperative ministry? Some segments of the ecumenical movement have advocated that. Certainly Christianity's testimony is not strengthened in the sight of the world by endlessly splintered groups, especially if there is acrimony involved. Complete unity is not an unequivocal goal, however. A true believer will not knowingly link with someone who merely claims to be Christian (2 Cor. 6:14). Each Christian and each congregation will have to decide, under the guidance of the Holy Spirit, how much agreement on details must exist for there to be union. There are, to be sure, situations in which union is not the most effective avenue to follow. While there are benefits in consolidation rather than duplication of efforts, studies have shown that several smaller groups can frequently minister more effectively and grow more rapidly than can a megachurch. As someone has said, "You never saw a McDonald's that seats a thousand people."

Whatever form the church may take, it is crucial to remember that it was established by our Lord (Matt. 16:18), and he gave it the task of continuing his ministry (Matt. 28:19–20). It is his body. Although we are not to worship it, only him, we should love it and be an active part of it.

Study Guide

Key Questions

1. What three images of the church bring to mind the members of the Trinity? What is the emphasis of each?
2. What are the four primary purposes or functions of the church?
3. What biblical principles can be utilized to construct an appropriate form of church government?
4. Why do some groups refer to the special practices of the church as sacraments, and other groups speak of them as ordinances?
5. In what three primary ways is baptism viewed?
6. How does the Lord's Supper tie together elements of the past, present, and future?

Bible Investigation

On the day of Pentecost, Peter, empowered by the Holy Spirit, preached to three thousand people who responded to his message to repent and be baptized. The beginning of the church can be traced to this event, which is recorded in Acts 2:37–47. What activities did the new converts share together? What evidence is there of worship, edification, evangelism, and social ministry? What attitudes characterized this fellowship? To what extent did these early believers demonstrate a unity of purpose and spirit? What result did their commitment bring? Would there have been the same outcome if the three thousand had simply gone home to worship God by themselves? To what extent does this example demonstrate that personal spiritual growth is nurtured by, or even dependent on, a corporate experience?

Personal Application

Suppose a co-worker discovers that you belong to and regularly attend a local church. She tells you that she is not interested in church because it is a place filled with hypocrites. She also expresses confusion over the many different denominations, which she regards as proof of the church's human origin. How might an understanding of the distinction between the universal and local church help her? Use Ephesians 4:1–16 to formulate a description of the universal church.

Which do you think is the better designation for the church—a "school for sinners" or a "society for saints"? Why? What types of people would find it difficult to be accepted and to serve in your church? Are there any invisible barriers which work to prevent certain individuals from attending your church or from fully participating in works of service?

For Further Thought

What is the nature of true spiritual unity? How can unity be achieved when there are differences in opinion? On what characteristics of mature believers does true unity depend?

The author makes the statement that in the church "the individual's opinion or conviction must always be made secondary to the good of the whole." Does this imply that decisions must be unanimous in order to maintain unity in the church? How does our individual opinion differ from our priesthood as a believer?

Suggested Additional Readings

Brown, Lavonn D. *The Life of the Church*. Nashville: Broadman, 1987.

Fletcher, Jesse C. *The Mission of the Church*. Nashville: Broadman, 1988.

Leonard, Bill J. *The Nature of the Church*. Nashville: Broadman, 1986.

12
And Finally

Humans have always been curious about the future. Because it is so uncertain, they attempt to determine the future from the markings on their palms, from tea leaves, crystal balls, Ouija boards, and other such devices. Persons who claim to be able to predict the future have been able to earn a handsome living thereby. Purporting to have a more scientific basis than fortune-telling, futurism has become a whole new discipline, its experts telling us what is supposedly coming in selected areas of human endeavor. The popularity of books like *Megatrends* also is an indication of people's interest in the future. The government's index of leading economic indicators is watched intently by persons who hope to secure their financial future. Among Christians, also, there are significant numbers who eagerly attend lectures on the last times and the signs of the times, hoping thereby to be able to prepare adequately for the future. Books like *The Late Great Planet Earth* sell millions of copies to persons eager for a clearer understanding of the Bible's teaching about what is to come.

I suspect that you also, at least to some degree, have an interest in the future. In this chapter we will look at some teachings about the future that are absolutely sure and true. They are going to come to pass. I can make that statement confidently because my source is God himself. The events to be discussed are all spoken of in the Bible.

Death

The first thing I can tell you with confidence is that you are going to die. I'm sorry to put it that bluntly, but the fact is that everyone, except for those who are alive when Christ returns, is going to die. The writer of the Letter to the Hebrews tells us that "man is destined to die once, and after that to face judgment" (9:27 NIV).

Death is not a pleasant thought for most people. So we look for different ways to avoid facing the reality of death. We use positive language to cloak the fact. For example, no one "dies" anymore. Instead, people "pass away." When I was young, there were undertakers; they were replaced by morticians and now by funeral directors. And whereas we formerly had graveyards, we now have cemeteries or even memorial parks. It really is not surprising that no one dies anymore, since we no longer have old people, who traditionally were the likeliest candidates for death. Instead, we have senior citizens or golden-agers. It all sounds so pleasant. We become senior citizens, and then we pass away, and the funeral director takes us to the memorial park. It sounds like going on a picnic, doesn't it? Yet, like an ostrich sticking its head in the ground, these attempts to ignore or deny the reality of death do not alter the fact, the inevitable fact, that it will come to everyone.

The Intermediate State

I can tell you something else that will definitely happen. After death you will be in a state of conscious existence, whether of blessedness or of misery. One of the questions that people often have at a funeral pertains to where the dead person is now or, as it is put, "Where is Grandma?" There are several places in Scripture which give indication of an intermediate state between life here and the final state of heaven or hell. Jesus said to the penitent thief on the cross, "I tell you the truth, today you will be with me in paradise" (Luke 23:43 NIV). Paul spoke of being "away from the body and at home with the Lord" (2 Cor. 5:8–9; see also Phil. 1:21–26). Finally, we note the parable of the rich man and Lazarus: both were in a conscious state, separated from one another and unable to pass across the gulf between them (Luke 16:19–31).

The Bible tells us little more about the intermediate state. Exactly where we will be or what our situation will be like is not spelled out. Our condition will in some ways be incomplete, since the resurrection will not yet have taken place; we will not yet have our resurrection bodies. Since Jesus said, "Today you will be with me . . . ," it appears that believers will experience the actual presence of the Lord, in other words, heaven, but not as fully as will be the case after the resurrection. Similarly, unbelievers will be in hell, but it will be less fully experienced than after the resurrection.

There are some Christians who believe that between death and resurrection we will simply repose in a state of unconsciousness, which they term "soul sleep." They base this idea upon a number of passages which speak of "sleep." This term, however, is merely an expression used of death (a euphemism, if you please). There also are some who hold that upon death we will go to a place of purging and punishment (usually referred to as purgatory). There is, however, in our Bible, no reference supporting this view.

The Second Coming

A third thing that I can tell you with certainty regarding the future is that Jesus Christ is coming again. Here we are not talking about something that will happen to each of us individually, but an event that will have universal consequences. When Jesus was readying his disciples for his departure, he told them that he was going to prepare a place for them, but that he would come again and would receive them to himself (John 14:2–3). At Jesus' ascension this promise was repeated by two men in white apparel (presumably angels): "This same Jesus . . . shall so come in like manner as ye have seen him go into heaven" (Acts 1:11 KJV). The message is repeated numerous other times, both in Jesus' teaching (e.g., Matt. 24:23–31; 25:31) and in the instruction given by Paul and other New Testament writers (e.g., 1 Thess. 4:13–18).

It is important to bear in mind that Jesus' second coming will be in the same form and manner as his departure (Acts 1:11). Thus it will be visible, personal, and bodily. There are those who hold that Jesus has already returned secretly. Some even believe that Jesus fulfilled this promise at Pentecost with the coming of the Holy Spirit. In both of these views there is no future return of Christ to wait for. Notice, however, that Jesus seemed to be referring to two different things when he spoke of his second coming and the coming of the Holy Spirit, which would require his going away (John 14:26; 16:7). Further, the descriptions of his return leave little doubt that it will be public and easily recognizable (e.g., 1 Thess. 4:16).

Another significant feature of the second coming is its surprise nature. It will be without warning; the time is unknown to everyone. Indeed, even Jesus himself during his earthly life did not know the time of his return (Matt. 24:36). Consequently, there will be many who, given to procrastination, will not be ready for his second coming, as Jesus taught in the parable of the wise and foolish virgins (Matt. 25:1–13). It is important that we have our houses in order, that we be living as if Jesus might return at any time. Diligence, watchfulness, and hope are the proper responses to the truth of Jesus' future coming.

The return of Christ will be the occasion of the resurrection of all believers. Those who have died will be raised from the dead; then those who are still alive will be caught up into the air to meet him. It will be a glorious time of victory. We are not told the exact nature of the body which we will have in the resurrection, although Paul does tell us it will be "a spiritual body" (1 Cor. 15:42–50), as contrasted with the physical body which we now have. It will have some point of continuity with our present body, but will not be merely a continuation of it. We will have a perfected body, free from death, pain, and deterioration (what Paul calls "corruption," vv. 42, 50, 53–54 KJV). This will be the stage of our completeness. For the intermediate state, of which we spoke earlier, is not the realization of the salvation of the full person. Our new spiritual body will entail leaving behind not only the aches and pains and griefs of this body, but the propensity to sin which also so fully afflicts us.

The Final Judgment

When Christ returns, there will be a great time of judgment. Christ will sit upon his throne and judge all the nations of the earth, everyone who has ever lived. There will be a definite and clear separation of the human race into two groups: those who have believed in Jesus Christ, and those who have not. Jesus likens this event to a shepherd's separating sheep and goats from one another (Matt. 25:32–33). There will be only one issue, namely, how people have related to him. Those who have been true believers and followers will receive eternal life; the others, eternal death. Some who will claim to have known Christ and expect to be admitted to heaven will be turned away with the words, "I never knew you" (Matt. 7:23). Jesus indicated that faith will be measured by the way we have lived (Matt. 25:31–46). We are reminded here of James's "Faith without deeds is dead" (James 2:26 NIV).

The final judgment will be a trial unlike any ever held before. In the courtroom trials of our experience there is a struggle to establish the exact truth. Witnesses are called and interrogated. Lawyers make their arguments. The process is sometimes lengthy and fraught with uncertainty. Doubts may still linger in the mind of the public as to whether the jury reached the right conclusion. This will not be the case with the final judgment, however. There every piece of information will be available, and no secrets can be covered. In his infinite knowledge and wisdom, the judge will rule infallibly.

The judgment that is coming is as certain as death (Heb. 9:27). To some this is a frightening thought, for they are not proud of how they have conducted their lives. They fear what will be uncovered and what the verdict will be. The idea of judgment stirs anxiety in their hearts, and so they frequently ignore the idea completely. For believers, however, there need be no such fear. In fact, believers will look forward to the judgment as a time when the truth will be made known and justice done. Their life of trust in Christ will be vindicated. The judgment will be something like an examination in school. For students who have not prepared adequately, this is a frightening prospect, for they fear that their ignorance of the subject will be revealed. On the other hand, students who have carefully and diligently prepared look forward to the opportunity to demonstrate what they have learned. So it is with the true believer and the final judgment.

Heaven and Hell

According to Matthew 25, we will be sent from the judgment to either the presence of God or eternal fire (vv. 34, 41). We will be consigned either to heaven or to hell, depending upon the outcome of the judgment. This is the place where we will spend all of eternity.

The most significant feature of heaven is that it will be the presence of God. Note that in the verses just cited there is a significant difference. The wicked are told, "*Depart from me*, you who are cursed, into the eternal fire prepared for the devil and his angels" (v. 41 NIV, italics added). The true followers, however, are bidden, "*Come*, you who are blessed by my Father; take your inheritance, the kingdom prepared for you since the creation of the world" (v. 34 NIV, italics added). The difference between the place of blessedness and the place of cursedness is the presence of the Lord in the former and his absence from the latter.

Sometimes we think of heaven as a place in which the very best of what we desire here on earth will be ours. We will enjoy feasting (with no worries about fats, cholesterol, triglycerides, sodium, or calories). We will live in mansions whose luxury will be proportional to the faithfulness which we have shown to the Lord. The splendor of heaven will be evident in its gold streets and various features of the decor. This, however, is in a very real sense a worldly notion: heaven is simply the fulfilment of our selfish earthly desires. But we will have been completely transformed by then into the likeness of Christ for which we were destined. There are indications that the satisfactions of this earthly life will be left behind as trivial (1 Cor. 2:9). The pictures of heaven as furnished with gold and precious stones are merely attempts to describe it in terms that make some sense to us now.

The Bible's few glimpses of heaven suggest that what goes on there is praise and worship of the Lord. The angels and seraphs are pictured as engaged in these activities. It will be our enjoyment of the Lord, not of ourselves and earthly pleasures, that will make it heaven. There will also be varying rewards. Although salvation does not admit of degrees (depending strictly on faith in Christ, it is something that a person either has or does not have), there will be degrees of rewards corresponding to the faithfulness with which we have served Christ. It is not clear just how these rewards will differ. The popular conception is that there will be externally different circumstances: one person will have a bigger mansion than another. The few glimpses we are afforded of heaven give no such hint, however. All of its citizens are engaged in the same activity. It may be that some persons will have a greater sensitivity to and appreciation of the joys of heaven, and so will have a higher enjoyment of them, just as concertgoers experience their own unique degree of pleasure. This, of course, is speculation. It does appear unlikely, however, that we will be given continual reminders throughout eternity of what things might have been like if we had only been a bit more faithful, like the next person. And, since all sorrows will be removed (Rev. 21:4), it seems unlikely that we will be aware of loved ones who are not there in heaven.

Hell, on the other hand, is a place of endless punishment and anguish, everlasting separation from the God by and for whom we were made, and whose true glory and beauty everyone will finally realize. There are different images of hell, including fire (Mark 9:43–49) and outer darkness (Matt. 22:13; 25:30), but it appears that these are primarily images used to convey a greater truth, since fire and darkness do not exist together. There are worse pains than physical pain, and perhaps the most agonizing of all is the psychological suffering related to the awful fact of loneliness. Throughout all eternity unbelievers, having seen how wonderful God is, will have to live with the sense that they are without him for whose fellowship they were created. Take the sorrow felt at the loss of a loved one, multiply it many times over, add the fact that time will not heal this hurt, and you have a bit of a feeling of what hell will be like.

Another aspect of hell is that there is no deliverance from one's sinful nature. If part of what heaven means is that there will be spiritual perfection, then hell means being left with one's evil self for all eternity with no hope for purification.

Heaven and hell are unending. Some have sought to argue that the suffering of hell does not go on eternally. The person will eventually die or cease to be, and that is eternal death, a permanent, unchanging state. It is important to observe the parallel, however, between eternal punishment (not eternal death) and eternal life in Matthew 25:46. Jesus uses the same adjective in each case and in exactly the same construction. If the life which the righteous receive is everlasting in duration, so must be the punishment which the unrighteous receive. Although we may not find the idea of everlasting punishment pleasant, it appears to be clearly taught in the Bible and by our Lord himself.

God's sending those who reject him to punishment which must continue forever may appear to some to be an awful act of vengeance. We need to bear in mind two things, however. One is that God's creating human beings in such a fashion that they can enjoy everlasting fellowship with him logically means that they are of such a nature that they can also be subject to everlasting suffering. They are not of such a nature that they will simply wear out or fade away. The other important fact is that in a sense God does not send anyone to hell. He has made provision for all to be saved, and invites all to come to him. It is not his desire to see any persons perish for their sins (2 Pet. 3:9). In a real sense, all who go to hell have sent themselves there, having chosen not to accept God's provision for salvation. As C. S. Lewis has put it, throughout life the sinner seeks to live independently of God, and in effect says, "Go away and leave me alone." Hell is God's finally and reluctantly giving sinners what they have insisted upon.

The Millennium and the Tribulation

Two more matters need to be dealt with. One is the question of the millennium. Does the Bible teach that Christ will reign bodily over this earth for what is represented as one thousand years, which, if not necessarily exact, certainly indicates a substantial period of time? Some have held that the "thousand years" mentioned in Revelation 20:4–6 is nothing more than a symbol of the totality of the Lord's victory over evil (amillennialism).

Their explanation of the two resurrections at the beginning and the end of the thousand years as being spiritual and physical respectively is difficult to maintain, for the two events are described identically. Others have maintained that the millennium will come to pass by the gradual conversion of the world through the preaching of the gospel; thus the kingdom of God is increasingly present even though Christ himself is not on earth (postmillennialism). This view seems unlikely, since the world does not appear to be increasingly turning to Christ. The premillennial view, that Christ will return personally to earth to set up his kingdom, fits best the relevant passages of Scripture, including the Old Testament prophecies about the conditions of peace which will someday prevail (e.g., Isa. 11:6–9).

One final issue is the tribulation. There are biblical passages which tell about a time of great anguish which will occur in connection with the second coming (e.g., Matt. 24:4–31). Christians have asked for some time whether the church will go through this tribulation or be removed ("raptured") from the world prior to it. One view holds that Jesus will come beforehand to take the church out of the world and then will return with the church at the end of the tribulation; another view maintains that the church will have to go through the tribulation. The use of the term *elect* in Matthew 24 (vv. 22, 24, 31) suggests that the church will be present during the tribulation. Furthermore, there is no firm evidence that the second coming will occur in two stages. Finally, the Greek in 1 Thessalonians 4:17 which is cited as evidence that the church will be caught away actually signifies that the church will "meet" the Lord in the air. This term is used elsewhere in the New Testament (Matt. 25:6 and Acts 28:15) of welcoming parties that go out to meet someone who is being honored and then return with him to where they came from. This is what believers will do when Christ comes back to earth.

Tragically, the doctrines of the last things have sometimes been the subject of dispute and even the cause of division within the church. They are, instead, to serve as encouragement and comfort to believers (1 Thess. 4:18). It is important to keep that purpose in mind and to enjoy the blessings of these wonderful truths.

Study Guide

Key Questions

1. According to the Bible, what events are certain to happen in the future?
2. What biblical evidence is there for "soul sleep" and purgatory?
3. In what manner will Christ return?
4. What other events will happen at the time of Christ's return?
5. Should the final judgment be feared? Why or why not?
6. What are the basic features of the biblical picture of heaven and hell?

Bible Investigation

In recent times many individuals have applied various interpretive schemes to prophetic portions of Scripture and proposed specific scenarios for the end times. It appears from these efforts that the primary purpose of prophecy is to foretell the future, and thus to satisfy our curiosity as to what will happen at the culmination of the world.

Carefully read 1 Corinthians 14:1–5 and 22–25. What is the purpose of prophecy according to this chapter? According to 1 Thessalonians 4:13–18 and 2 Peter 3, in what ways should knowing a portion of God's plan for the future affect one's life?

Personal Application

Scripture is clear concerning the certainty of a future judgment. At that time "there will be a definite and clear separation of the human race into two groups: those who have believed in Jesus Christ, and those who have not." Both Matthew 7:15–23 and 25:31–46 give clear indications concerning the nature of true belief in Christ. In light of Jesus' teachings here, is it possible to be assured of a place in heaven if there are no visible evidences of a relationship with Christ in one's life?

For Further Thought

Understanding prophecy to be a timeless injunction to "live holy and godly lives as you look forward to the day of God and speed its coming" (2 Pet. 3:11–12 NIV) should result in a careful search to discover in the prophets of old the message that God has for his people today. Skim through a shorter book of prophecy, such as Malachi, Micah, or Amos, to discover its main ideas. (A version of the Bible that includes subheads will be very helpful.) If you do this with more than one book, you will notice a similarity of themes. When you encounter a passage that is futuristic, consider whether the general time of its fulfilment is clearly indicated. Sometimes it is difficult to determine whether what was being predicted applied to the immediate or the distant future. In either case, assess the effect of such a prediction on the original hearers of the prophecy. What purpose did this prediction serve? Does it really matter whether we can determine the precise circumstances which have fulfilled or will fulfil the prophecy? Should that make any difference in believers' lives today?

Suggested Additional Readings

Archer, Gleason L., Jr.; Paul D. Feinberg; Douglas J. Moo; and Richard R. Reiter. *The Rapture: Pre-, Mid-, or Post-Tribulational?* Grand Rapids: Zondervan, 1984.

Ashcraft, Morris. *The Christian Hope.* Nashville: Broadman, 1988.

Clouse, Robert G., ed. *The Meaning of the Millennium.* Winona Lake, Ind.: BMH Books, 1978.

Erickson, Millard J. *Contemporary Options in Eschatology: A Study of the Millennium.* Grand Rapids: Baker, 1977.

13

Epilog:
The Difference
Belief Makes

We come now to the question with which we began our discussion: Does it matter what I believe? In this epilog we will retrace to some extent our steps in this brief study to see what difference our beliefs make or should make in specific areas.

If we believe that the Bible is God's message to us, we will take very seriously what it says. Suppose that you found what you believed to be an authentic old map indicating where pirates had hidden stolen treasure. In hope of rich rewards, you would probably study the map in great detail and act on it. As Christians who believe that the Bible directs us to eternal life, our fervor will be even greater, for the Bible speaks of eternal, not temporary, treasures.

We will also take the Bible personally. The psalmist said, "Thy word is a lamp to my feet and a light to my path" (119:105). As believers, we will let the Bible's teachings and values shape our lives, our ways of thinking and acting. The way we regard other human beings will reflect our understanding of the Bible: we will see them not as objects, but as persons created in God's image and valuable to him. While the Bible does not give us detailed instructions on how to conduct a business, it does give us guidance as to the values and ethics we should bring to our occupation. It tells us what are appropriate goals for life and where to focus our activity. It tells us what the church is to be about and how to measure its success.

If we believe the Bible is the Word of God, our attitudes will be shaped by what God has said, not by what the world about us tells us are important objectives to pursue and proper ways to think. We will be like the psalmist, who dwelt upon the law of the Lord and found delight in his teachings (Ps. 1).

We will, on the other hand, bear in mind that God has given us a general revelation as well. We will not look to the Bible to give us the answers in fields like chemistry and economics. We will not expect it to give us direction as to what crop to plant, or what automobile to buy, although it will give some general principles to guide us. We will not expect it to do less than it is intended to do, but neither will we expect it to do more or inappropriate things.

If we have correctly understood God, we will recognize that he is the source of all creation and the center of all existence. We have been created by him and exist for his sake and his glory, not he for ours. We will always repeat the prayer of Samuel: "Speak, LORD, for your servant is listening" (1 Sam. 3:9–10 NIV). We will always be ready to hear and to do what he calls upon us to do. We will never suffer from an "inverted theology" which says, in effect, "Listen, Lord, for your servant is speaking." We will not put ourselves in God's place and him in ours, so that we become demanding and seek to make him do our will. Nor will we expect him to do only what seems to us to be pleasant and right. We will recognize that he is Lord of all, including us.

In addition, if we correctly understand God, we will not fear or be lonely. We will recognize that when we think we are alone or in danger, he is always there, knowing our situation and caring for us. There is nothing in our lives or anywhere in the universe that God does not know about, or has not planned from all eternity. We will also recognize that nothing is too hard for God. We can entrust him with all of our hopes and dreams, knowing that he is perfectly wise, and that whatever he does and allows to happen will actually be best for us in the long run. Because he is God, we will desire to see his will done, not ours.

Knowing that God is the Creator of all will give us a special respect and regard for the world about us. It is not simply something that is there. It has come from his hand; as such it is valuable and, in a derivative sense, even sacred. Accordingly, we will practice a good stewardship of the environment, preserving and protecting it both for its own sake and for the sake of future generations.

Furthermore, if we have correctly understood the way in which God acts, we will not expect him to accomplish all of his work in a direct, miraculous fashion. Just as he used his servants to do his work in biblical times, so will he work through us as we make plans, utilize our abilities, and carry on our efforts in dependence upon him. We will neither presume that we can do these things apart from him, nor will we expect him to perform miracles if we neglect his more general provisions for our needs. We will fully utilize such provisions as medical science, recognizing that God is the source of medical science; at the same time we will acknowledge that he can, if he wills, do that which is, from a human perspective, impossible.

Recognition that God is the Creator of everything will spare us from the sense of hopelessness and despair that is so common in our world. For us, life can never be merely a maze or a meaningless wandering. Someone supremely wise and powerful is in control, and is planning our days and our ways. It is a comfort to us to know that whatever happens in our lives is not the result of chance factors.

A proper understanding of human nature will bear upon our attitudes and actions toward others. If we have fully understood the biblical teaching here, we will not regard anyone as worthless or undesirable; rather, we will see that each individual has been created in the image and likeness of God, and is therefore of supreme value to him. We will never be able to take lightly the loss of a human life, no matter how insignificant the person may seem, since every one is precious in the sight of God. To help others find such fulfilment in a relationship with God as we ourselves have found will be one of our primary concerns.

We will also understand that humans are unitary beings. Therefore, all of human nature—the physical, the psychological, and the spiritual—is important, both to God and to us. Inasmuch as the physical body is in its original state good, not evil, it is not something to be shunned. Spirituality, then, is not a matter of fleeing from the body, but of bringing all of one's being, physical as well as spiritual, into conformity with the will of God.

A correct understanding of sin will keep us on guard against it. Sin, as we have seen, includes far more than wrong actions; it is, in fact, defined as any lack of conformity to God's will, which in turn is an expression of his nature. Thus it is possible to sin not only through rebellion and disobedience, but also through neglect, indifference, or even proper action from the wrong motivation. Moreover, sin extends to our thoughts and attitudes, as Jesus pointed out in the Sermon on the Mount (Matt. 5:21–30).

Given this understanding, we will be skeptical about "positive thinking," which minimizes human sinfulness and assumes that anything is possible if we simply have correct attitudes and apply ourselves. We also will be skeptical about societal plans which assume that humans are basically unselfish and perfectible. And we will scrutinize our own actions and thoughts, knowing how easily we may deceive ourselves.

Another element of a correct understanding is that sin is universal, that all persons sin. Knowing that every individual is therefore under the condemnation of God will lend impetus and urgency to the evangelistic task.

All of this awareness of sin and its consequences would be a disturbing and even frightening prospect if it were not for the biblical teaching about Christ. As we reflect upon the truth of who Jesus is, our awe of and love for our Lord will grow. The perfect, fully divine Second Person of the Trinity was willing to leave the splendors and glory of heaven to come to earth and give his life for us. In him who loved and died for those who did not love him we will recognize the perfect example of true love. We will also be certain not to neglect in any respect the picture of Jesus as fully God and fully human. We will find comfort in knowing that Jesus was as human as we are. Indeed, he was in certain respects more human than we; he therefore can understand every temptation, sorrow, and pain, as well as every joy, that we experience. We will be filled with gratitude, which will in turn cause us to want to serve and obey him in all that we do.

We will understand that Jesus is also the perfect example after whom to pattern our lives, the ultimate model and ideal of true humanity. We will strive to emulate him, not some mere human, for even the noblest Christians are not in the same class with him. He is in a class by himself. Because he alone was God in human form, only he can save. There is no one else in whom our faith is to be placed.

We will also recognize that Jesus is a person of unique compassion. He did not think of his disciples as slaves; rather, he called them his friends (John 15:15). He wanted them to think of him not as a slave driver, but as their friend. We, then, should not live in fear of him, but should carry the greatest of respect for him, and desire to do all that we can to please him.

It is essential that we understand precisely how Jesus

saves us. He has made salvation available to us, not simply by giving us an example of how we can live perfectly, or a powerful inducement to return to God, but by actually taking our place and bearing the penalty for sin which we should have borne. Consequently, Good Friday will be more than just another religious holiday for us. It will evoke both a deep awareness of the scope of God's love and a sense of wonder at our being relieved of doing what he has now done for us. Though we ourselves should have been there upon the cross, we have been spared because of his sacrifice.

A correct understanding of the Holy Spirit will make him more personal and more real to us. He will not be simply a vague force, or an eery unknown activity in our lives. He will be understood to be a person, as real and as fully divine as the Father and the Son, someone with whom we can relate, and who is deserving of our praise and worship, someone to whom we can pray and upon whom we can rely. We will realize that there is room for neither pride in the gifts which we have, nor envy of those having seemingly greater gifts than ours, since the Holy Spirit confers such gifts upon whomever he chooses so to honor. We will learn increasingly to trust him as our guide in life, and to place our confidence in him to enable our service, knowing that it is he who will do the convicting of unbelievers regarding sin, righteousness, and judgment, and who will give effectiveness to our efforts, just as he did with Peter's Pentecost sermon. We will more and more realize that what we accomplish in service is his doing rather than ours. Just as he gave unusual blessing to the ministry of the early church, so he also will enable us to accomplish what we think to be beyond our capabilities (provided, of course, that it is really something that he wills for us to do). We will seek to let him fill our lives increasingly. Though we already have all of him, we will continually yield more of our lives to him. Our personal devotional time will include prayers to him, both asking him to take and granting him control of our lives.

Our amazement at salvation will never cease to grow as we reflect on the meaning of what has happened to us and is continuing to happen. A true understanding of the sin in ourselves and in the human race in general could bring us to a point of despair. Many have become cynics in the face of their own propensity for doing the wrong thing and the human race's history of warfare and violence. Our despair upon realizing we can never be good enough on our own is overcome, however, when we realize that God has already provided the righteousness of Christ, and that it becomes ours when we become identified with him in faith. To have our guilt wiped away and our sins canceled by Christ's perfect righteousness is surely not a cause for pride, but for continuing gratitude. Although we may find it difficult to believe that we do not have to pay the penalty for our sins, it is the truth nonetheless.

The sense of frustration which sensitive and concerned persons feel over their own sinful nature can be overcome by a proper understanding of the doctrine of regeneration. The person really is made new, with a new impulse and new vitality imparted. This new life continues to grow and develop, in some cases quite rapidly, in others more gradually, but nonetheless genuinely. We do not have to reform ourselves by resolution and effort, for we have the power of God within us. We need not come to God fearfully, as those who deserve punishment, but as those who are now his restored children. Like the prodigal son of whom Jesus told, we are the cause of the Father's rejoicing. He really loves us, unconditionally.

We can have the assurance that we are constantly being changed for the better. The work begun continues. Whether or not we feel good about ourselves on a given day, God is at work within us. And we can have the assurance that one day the process will be complete. Every physical imperfection we have had in this life will be removed; beyond that, the old nature with its tendency to sin will be gone. We will be like God and will never again experience temptation.

There is also the assurance that we are not called to be solitary believers, for we are part of the body of Christ, the church. While each of us lacks much of what is needed for fulfilling Christ's expectation of us, we are part of a body in which all of the necessary gifts are present. What we cannot do alone, we can do collectively. The encouragement, instruction, and correction offered by other believers are a powerful incentive to our lives. Teaming with others makes possible the service of which we are not capable alone. We cannot personally go everywhere in fulfilment of Jesus' commission, but the church collectively certainly can. In addition, within the church we can worship God with others and share our burdens and our strengths. God has provided the church to pray for us at those times when we feel too spiritually weak to pray.

Finally, most of us have a natural curiosity about the future. Sometimes this takes the form of a sense of anticipation of what might be, sometimes it reflects an anxiety about what could come to pass. No one, in the final analysis, can predict the future, except for relatively short periods, in limited areas, and in considerable generality. The Bible, however, gives us a more specific understanding of what is to come, both for us as individuals and for the whole creation. Human experience tells us that death is sure for each of us. But what lies beyond that? The Bible tells us that death is but the transition to an eternal existence. Those who have died in Christ will go to be in the presence of God, while those who have died unbelieving will be separated from him. Then will come Christ's return, which will entail the resurrection of all with a perfected body, the final judgment, and the consignment of believers to endless presence with God and of unbelievers to interminable separation from him.

This is a source of immense comfort to us. We can

know that Christian loved ones who have died are now in the presence of the Lord. We can be assured that there is a judgment coming in which the apparent inequities of life will be righted. And we can know that our salvation can never be lost. Paul urged his readers to comfort one another with the truth of the second coming (1 Thess. 4:13–18), something we should do as well. That the final state is everlasting and unchangeable should motivate us to make sure we have placed our trust in Christ, and to strenuously urge non-Christians to accept him.

Study Guide

Key Questions

1. Do you believe the Bible is really God's message to us? Give as many reasons as you can to support your answer.

2. If we truly believe that the Bible is God's message to us, then we will allow its teachings and its values to shape our beliefs, attitudes, and behavior. Complete the following "if . . . then" statements to reflect specific ways in which the Bible might mold our lives. Try to complete each statement in more than one way:

> If it is true that the Bible directs us to eternal life, then. . . .
>
> If we recognize that God is the source of all creation, then. . . .
>
> If we know God to be sovereign, then. . . .
>
> If we regard Scripture as God's guide for our lives, then. . . .
>
> If we think of ourselves as having been created in God's image, then. . . .
>
> If we have a proper understanding of our own sin, then. . . .
>
> If we grasp the truth of who Jesus is, then. . . .
>
> If we understand the person of the Holy Spirit, then. . . .
>
> If we know how our salvation is accomplished, then. . . .
>
> If we consider the church to be Christians functioning together as the body of Christ, then. . . .
>
> If we have confidence concerning the return of Christ, then. . . .
>
> If we truly find our fulfilment in our relationship with God, then. . . .

Bible Investigation

Carefully read Psalm 1. Using the analogy of the tree in this passage, list the benefits which come to a person whose "delight is in the law of the LORD."

Read through Psalm 119, taking note of the various ways in which a proper understanding of God's Word shapes one's whole life—intellect, attitudes, and behavior.

Personal Application

The main assertion of this book is that it really does matter what one believes, because our beliefs determine our actions and indeed the whole pattern of our lives. The ultimate goal of all biblical learning is to apply our beliefs to our own specific situation. Regular devotional reading of Scripture becomes very important in this regard. As we study a particular portion of Scripture, asking a series of pointed questions will help us apply its message to our own situation: "What precisely does this passage have to say about my relationship with God? my relationship with other believers? my relationship to unbelievers? my responsibility for myself? How can taking this text to heart improve my personal outlook, attitude, spiritual growth, endeavors to avoid defeat and to achieve maturity?" Choose a favorite Bible passage and apply it to your own life, using these questions as a guide.

For Further Thought

Recent polls indicate that most Americans claim belief in the existence of God, yet this belief does little to shape their ways of thinking and living. (To these individuals, contrary to the main idea of this book, it really does *not* seem to matter what one believes!) Provide some evidence which supports this finding, and try to come up with some reasons why this is the case. What, then, is the basis of the attitudes and conduct of most people?

Read Ephesians 4. According to this chapter, what is the relationship between right belief and right action?

Teaching Suggestions

Chapter 1. Does It Matter What I Believe?

1. Write the following questions on the board before the beginning of the class: "What is my present attitude toward the study of doctrine; what factors lie behind this attitude? How much does what I believe matter? Isn't loving Jesus enough?" When the class members arrive, spend some time getting acquainted. Then ask for responses to the questions on the board.

2. After the class members have shared responses, point out what Jesus had to say about right beliefs (see Matt. 16:13–19) and about the relationship between them and right actions (see Luke 6:46–49; Matt. 7:21–23). Stress the conclusion that to be a disciple of Jesus, one must not only believe, but also *do* the things that he teaches.

If time permits, proceed through the "Bible Investigation" at the end of the chapter. Emphasize that Christians will be held accountable for knowing and applying what God has revealed to them through his Word.

3. Present in lecture style the three common objections to the study of doctrine. Summarize the responses which the text makes to these objections.

4. Point out that once we understand the importance of doctrine, we need to determine an appropriate starting point for the study of theology. Divide the class in half. Ask one group to defend the idea that we must begin by establishing on some

grounds other than the Bible the existence of God, and only then can we go on to other doctrines. Ask the other group to defend the idea that we should start with the assumption that the Bible is true revelation from God and then go on to examine what it says about him. See "For Further Thought" at the end of the chapter.

5. If time permits, consider the issue of unity as it is presented in the "Personal Application."

Chapter 2. When All Else Fails, Read the Instruction Book

1. Before class write the following question on the board: "In what ways has God revealed himself to humankind?" Make a list of the various responses. Then ask for volunteers to read a number of Scripture verses that will confirm and supplement the list: Psalm 19:1–4; Romans 1:19–20; Romans 2:14–16; Psalm 33:8–19; Jeremiah 18:1; Ezekiel 12:1; 1 Kings 18:36–39; John 1:14–18; 2 Peter 1:20–21; John 14:26.

Once the list is complete, ask the class members to suggest ways in which the various items on the list could be divided into two distinct groups. Accept the suggestions that are offered, and then point out that one possibility is to distinguish between means of revelation which are more general, being available to all humans at all times (e.g., the revelation in creation, moral consciousness, and God's providence in history), and means of revelation which are more definite and specific (e.g., direct and indirect speech, miraculous demonstrations of power, Christ's incarnation, the writing of Scripture, and the guidance of the Holy Spirit). Having drawn this distinction, ask the class which of the various ways of communication makes it possible to preserve the others in such a way that they can be known and believed by everyone in all ages.

2. To identify the nature of God's work in and with Scripture, ask what role God played in creating and preserving the Bible. Using material from the text, explain the concept of inspiration. Then ask what role God plays in interpreting the Bible, and explain the concept of illumination. At this point discuss the "Personal Application" found at the end of the chapter. It will be helpful to stress the statement in the text that "this work of the Holy Spirit [illumination] in no way contradicts

what careful study of the biblical text discloses, nor is it a short-cut making such study unnecessary. The Spirit illumines our understanding, and the more knowledge we can acquire, the more he has to work with."

3. In a brainstorming session have the class suggest various possible sources of spiritual truth: feelings, tradition, reason, experience, God's Word. Ask the class which source is most dependable and why.

4. Conclude with a discussion of any of the issues raised in the "Bible Investigation" or "For Further Thought."

Chapter 3. Who's the Boss?

1. Write the following question on the board: "If it's true that most Americans believe in God, why don't they govern their lives by what he has to say?" After some discussion, explain that people who have an uninformed or misinformed concept of God are ill equipped to take him seriously. (You may wish to use "For Further Thought" as additional introductory material for this lesson.)

2. Hold a brainstorming session to compile a list of the attributes of God. As you enter the list on the board, ask the class members to suggest Scripture verses that associate God with each particular attribute. Supply from the text the attributes that are missed.

Point out that a misconception of God arises when one or more of these characteristics are emphasized over and above the others. Discuss which elements are missing from the concept of God as an indulgent grandfather, a celestial highway patrolman, a cosmic chess player. To dispel the misconception that the God of the Old Testament is different from the God of the New Testament, use part 2 of the "Bible Investigation" at the end of the chapter.

3. To emphasize how a correct understanding of the nature of God should lead to a proper response to him, have the class do the activity suggested under "Personal Application." Have each class member choose an attribute from the board and write down an implication, expectation, or consequence that follows from it. Then collect and randomly redistribute the responses.

4. Lead a discussion of the "inverted theology" described in the text. Use part 1 of the "Bible Investigation" to draw out

the conclusion that God will accomplish his will despite our poor or even wrong choices.

5. If time permits, use material from the text to discuss the nature of the Trinity. Conclude the session by having volunteers praise the individual members of the Trinity for their unique functions.

Chapter 4. What's Going On Around Here?

1. Write the following question on the board: "In what ways does God continuously exercise care over his creation?" After initial responses are given, read a variety of Scripture references that will confirm and add to them: Nehemiah 9:6; Colossians 1:17; Matthew 10:29; Psalm 121; Psalm 139:16; Matthew 5:45; Daniel 4:24–25; 1 Corinthians 4:6–7; Isaiah 37:26; Isaiah 46:10–11; Proverbs 19:21. Explain how the providence of God is demonstrated in his personal care of the created order and its people, his governing of history, and the working out of his all-inclusive divine purpose.

2. Discuss to what extent God takes special care to protect Christians from the terrible things that would otherwise happen. Use the "Bible Investigation" at the end of the chapter to study Psalm 91. Draw out the conclusion that while God has not granted Christians special immunity from the pain, sorrow, and death that are a part of this sinful world, in his sovereignty he can bring blessings out of bad situations.

3. Discuss whether God's having a predetermined plan for what happens on earth means that Christians must diligently search for the one best course of action which will put them at the very center of his will. Proceeding through the "Personal Application," draw out the conclusion that since we cannot know in detail what God's plan is, we should make our decisions on the basis of the general principles he has revealed in his Word. Thus we can be confident that we are able to make decisions which are pleasing to God, and that even if we err, God can still accomplish his will through (and even in spite of) us.

4. To show how a correct understanding of God's providential activity should affect how we live, summarize the items listed in the section entitled "A Proper Response to God's Work." Be sure to include the role that prayer plays in accomplishing what

God has planned. A helpful illustration here is the well-known speaker who, at the dawn of each new day, inquired of God, "Lord, what is it that you are going to do in your world today? Whatever it is, may I please get in on it?"

5. Conclude the session with a discussion of Habakkuk's struggle to understand God's work in the world. See "For Further Thought."

Chapter 5. Who Am I?

1. Write the following questions on the board: "What does it mean to be human? Under what circumstances does a person become less than fully human?" After some discussion, propose the idea that people are less than fully human—less than their highest and best—if they are not fulfilling the purpose for which they were created. Ask how this explains the failure of many human pursuits to bring lasting fulfilment.

2. Focus on the scriptural teaching that we have purpose and value because we have been created by God in his image. Ask the class whether God's conferring special value on human beings eliminates the need to work on raising low self-esteem. How ought a biblically correct understanding of ourselves to affect our self-concept?

Proceed through the "Bible Investigation" and part 1 of the "Personal Application." Elaborate on the idea that since only humans have been made in God's image, they have a unique place of infinite worth within the creation. Using the text, enumerate some of the special benefits that can be enjoyed because of this endowment from God.

3. Discuss the idea that to be fully human is to be genuinely free. Ask the class to define the nature of true freedom and to suggest ways in which freedom can become restricted or even lost. Conclude that persons who try to exercise their freedom independently of God or contrary to his will find that slavery rather than freedom is the result.

Point out that true freedom is the ability to do and become that which the Creator intended us to do and be. Ask the class for examples of ways in which we can be prevented from realizing our fullest potential. Encourage them to describe something that has inhibited them from becoming what God intends them to be. Discuss correctives that can be applied—in families, in churches, in schools, in society—to make sure all of us reach our full potential.

4. Stress the idea that what we think about ourselves greatly affects how we live. If we value ourselves in the same way God does, we will strive to protect life and to prevent whatever may make it difficult or painful. Conclude with a brainstorming session on what implications a proper understanding of humanity has for our lives. Include the issues raised in "For Further Thought."

Chapter 6. Whatever Became of Sin?

1. Provide a dictionary definition of the word *concupiscence*. Then read to the class the following paragraph from the works of John Calvin, the Reformation theologian. Practice reading the quotation ahead of time, so that it can be shared with a certain degree of dramatic flair:

> Original sin is seen to be a hereditary depravity and corruption of our nature, diffused into all parts of the soul. . . . Therefore those who have defined original sin as the lack of the original righteousness with which we should have been endowed, no doubt include, by implication, the whole fact of the matter, but they have not fully expressed the positive energy of this sin. For our nature is not merely bereft of good, but is so productive of every kind of evil that it cannot be inactive. Those who have called it concupiscence have used a word by no means wide of the mark, if it were added (and this is what many do not concede) that whatever is in man, from intellect to will, from the soul to the flesh, is all defiled and crammed with concupiscence; or, to sum it up briefly, that the whole man is in himself nothing but concupiscence. [*Institutes of the Christian Religion* 2.1, quoted in *Documents of the Christian Church*, ed. Henry S. Bettenson, 2d ed. (New York: Oxford University Press, 1963), 213]

Tell the class that the object in reading this excerpt is to contrast Calvin's grave view of sin with the way it is often viewed today. Then ask them to verbalize their own concepts of original sin. Refer to the sections in the text entitled "The Universality of Sin" and "The Human Predicament."

2. Ask the class members to formulate with the person sitting next to them a general definition of sin. As the various defini-

tions are shared, delineate the three main types of sin described in the text. Summarize by writing on the board and then discussing the definition that appears in the text: "Sin is any act, thought, or state that fails to conform to the moral and spiritual will of God."

3. Present the idea that even "good actions," or actions which fulfil the law of God, are sinful if done for the wrong motive. Make the application that even worship can become sinful under certain circumstances. Discuss the issues raised in the "Personal Application."

4. Use the "Bible Investigation" to study Psalm 51. Incorporate within the discussion the adverse effects of sin which are described in the section entitled "The Consequences of Sin."

5. Conclude the session by discussing the issues raised in either or both parts of "For Further Thought."

Chapter 7. Jesus—God and Man

1. Write the following questions on the board: "To what extent did having a human body limit Jesus from exercising certain divine prerogatives? When Jesus lived on earth, was he omnipresent (able to be everywhere at once)? omniscient (able to know everything in the past, present, and future)? omnipotent (able to do all things)?" After some discussion, use Philippians 2:5–11 to draw the conclusion that Jesus voluntarily assumed some limitations when he took the form of a man. (We know, for example, from Matt. 24:36 that he did not know when the second coming will occur.) Refer to the sections in the text entitled "The Humanity of Jesus" and "The Mystery." Ask the class how an understanding of and appreciation for the humanity of Jesus can help us to pray confidently. See Hebrews 4:14–16.

2. Divide the class into two groups. Each group is to formulate a defense of Jesus' deity. The first group will focus on Scripture passages which indicate what Jesus understood himself to be: Mark 2:1–12; Mark 2:23–28; John 8:58; John 10:24–39; Matthew 25:31–46; John 14:1–11; Matthew 26:63–64. The second group will focus on Scripture passages indicating what others understood him to be: Luke 9:18–20; John 1:1–34; John 20:26–28; Colossians 1:13–23; Colossians 2:8–10; Hebrews 1; 1 John 5:20.

3. Conclude the session with the "Personal Application" at the end of the chapter. The writing assignment can be done either on an individual basis, with volunteers sharing their paragraphs afterward, or as a group project using the chalkboard.

Chapter 8. Prophet and Priest and King

1. Write the following question on the board: "What do you think is the central theme of Jesus' teaching?" After some initial responses are suggested, refer to Mark 1:14–15; Matthew 4:17, 23; and Luke 4:42–43, and note what phrase recurs there. Utilize the questions and suggested Scripture references in "For Further Thought" to determine the nature of the kingdom of God.

Ask in what sense Christ's kingly rule is a present reality (see Luke 17:20–21; Matt. 6:33) and in what sense it is a future hope (see Luke 23:42; Matt. 16:28). Elaborate on the idea that Jesus inaugurated the kingdom of God when he initiated his earthly ministry, but that it will not be fully consummated until his second coming.

2. Use the opening paragraphs of the chapter to introduce the threefold work of Christ in the roles of prophet, priest, and king. Then turn to the "Bible Investigation" to expand on these concepts.

3. Refer to John 1:18 and 14:9–10 as evidence that the Gospels present Jesus as a prophet. Compare the content of his teaching in Matthew 23:23–28; Mark 7:1–23; and Mark 13 with that of the prophets.

4. With the help of the material in the section entitled "Priest," present the various purposes of Christ's death: he paid the penalty for sin, defeated evil, demonstrated infinite love, and served as an example of the attitudes and behaviors God expects of us. Point out that only Jesus could have made the contribution that he did in his role as priest. He offered the ultimate sacrifice by his death on the cross.

5. Use the "Personal Application" to help the class spell out what would be an appropriate response to Jesus' ministry.

6. Conclude with a brainstorming session on ways that believers can make the reign of Christ an increasing reality.

Chapter 9. The Least-Known Member of the Trinity

1. Write the following question on the board: "What are the evidences of the activity of the Holy Spirit in the individual? in the church?" After some discussion, refer to Acts 1:8; 2:47; 4:32; and Galatians 5:22–23.

2. Hold a brainstorming session to compile a list of the attributes which reflect the deity of the Holy Spirit. Have the class members supply Scripture texts that support their suggestions. Use the following texts to fill in some of the attributes that are missed: Job 33:4; Psalm 139:7; Isaiah 40:13; John 14:26; Romans 8:2, 11; Romans 15:30; 1 Corinthians 2:10–12; 1 Corinthians 12:11; 1 John 5:7.

3. Work through the "Bible Investigation" to discover the primary role of the Holy Spirit and his relationship to the Son. Draw out the idea that the Holy Spirit was given to empower us to continue the work of Christ. The guidance of the Holy Spirit is tied to the lordship of Christ and the content of what God has revealed to us in the Bible.

4. Divide the class into two groups. Instruct the first group to study texts that describe the activity of the Holy Spirit during the Old Testament period: Genesis 1:2; Job 26:13; Isaiah 32:15; Exodus 31:3–5; Numbers 11:25; Deuteronomy 34:9; Judges 3:10; 6:34; 14:19; Ezekiel 2:2; 11:1, 5, 24; 2 Peter 1:20–21. Instruct the second group to study texts that describe the activity of the Holy Spirit during the New Testament period: John 14:16; John 14:26; 16:13–14; John 17:7–11; John 3:3, 5–8; Romans 8:1–17, 26; 1 Corinthians 12:7–31; Galatians 5:22–23; 2 Thessalonians 2:13. Have the two groups summarize their findings and then discuss the extent to which there is a continuity between the working of the Holy Spirit in the Old and New Testament periods.

5. Point out that the fruit of the Holy Spirit is intended for all Christians and has to do with character. The gifts of the Spirit, by comparison, are not intended for all Christians and have to do with abilities. Ask whether it is possible to have either the fruit of the Spirit without the gifts or the gifts without the fruit. Which is more important? Which fruit controls all the others? See 1 Corinthians 12:31–13:3.

6. If time permits, discuss some of the issues raised in the "Personal Application" or "For Further Thought."

7. Conclude the session by considering the role of the individual in producing the work of the Spirit. To show that the work of the Spirit is dependent on us, refer to Philippians 2:12–13; Colossians 1:29; and Hebrews 12:14. Have the class suggest ways we can properly respond to and work with the Spirit.

Chapter 10. So Great Salvation

1. Ask the class members to complete the following quiz:

Aspects of Salvation

Match the aspects of salvation with their definitions:

a. Adoption
b. Conversion
c. Faith
d. Glorification
e. Justification
f. Perseverance
g. Regeneration
h. Repentance
i. Sanctification
j. Union with Christ

_____ Making a complete about-face by turning to Christ

_____ Godly sorrow for sin and resolve to turn from it

_____ Belief and complete trust in Christ and his work as the basis of our relationship to God

_____ Identification with Christ in his atoning death as well as in his resurrection power

_____ The declaration that we have been restored to a state of righteousness in God's sight

_____ God's receiving the estranged sinner back into the relationship and benefits of being his child

_____ The work of the Holy Spirit in creating a new life in the person who repents and comes to Christ

_____ God's work of making the believer actually holy or good

_____ The genuine believer's being enabled by Christ to endure in the faith to the end

_____ The completion of our growth in godliness at the second coming of Christ

Use the material in the text to expand upon the definitions. Draw out the conclusion that salvation is a much more comprehensive experience than we often realize.

2. Ask the class members whether they agree or disagree with the statement that all born-again individuals should be able to identify a point in time when they were converted. After some discussion, explain that the purpose of this question is to consider whether salvation is a process or an event. Use the material in the text to point out that for some people conversion may involve a prolonged process of gradually coming to repentance and faith.

3. Focus on salvation as a process by considering such aspects as sanctification and glorification. Use the material in "For Further Thought" to investigate the past, present, and future elements of salvation.

4. Use the "Bible Investigation" to lead a discussion on the relationship between faith and works as they pertain to salvation. Emphasize that saving faith involves a level of personal trust _which results in acting upon what we believe._

5. If time permits, some of the class members might enjoy sharing the circumstances of their conversion.

6. Conclude the session by considering the need for preparation if we are to successfully share the gospel of salvation. Have on hand several different tracts for the class to examine while going through the "Personal Application."

Chapter 11. Christianity in the Collective Form

1. Write the following questions on the board: "Do I need to attend a church? Can't I worship God in my own private way? Is it possible to live out one's Christian life in isolation?" Stress that although salvation comes to us as individuals, our new life in Christ should not be restricted to that level. God intends each believer to be part of a community of faith. Consider the hallmark of Christian maturity, the fruit of the Spirit. None of these character traits—love, joy, peace, patience, kindness, goodness, faithfulness, gentleness, self-control—can be demonstrated in isolation! All must be cultivated within a continuing context of relationship.

2. Use the "Bible Investigation" to continue discussion on collectively experiencing spiritual growth. Refer to the material in the section entitled "The Purpose of the Church" to expand on the specific ways in which the church continues Christ's ministry. Ask whether the church today demonstrates the same unity of purpose and spirit as did the early church.

Also discuss the nature of the church by describing the images of the church suggested by the members of the Trinity: the people of God, the body of Christ, and the temple of the Holy Spirit. (See the material in the section entitled "Images of the Church.")

3. Distribute copies of your church constitution to each class member. Determine the type of organizational structure it exemplifies. Discuss whether your church does things "in a fitting and orderly way" (1 Cor. 14:40 NIV). How are decisions made? Are all individuals encouraged to reach their full potential in Christ (see Rom. 12 and 1 Cor. 12)? Is each person encouraged to approach God directly and be led by him (see Rom. 5:1–5; 1 Tim. 2:5; and Heb. 4:14–16)?

4. Discuss how your church views baptism and the Lord's Supper. Are they considered ordinances or sacraments?

5. As time permits, use the "Personal Application" and "For Further Thought" to lead discussions on exclusiveness and disunity in the church.

6. Conclude the session by returning the focus to the person who created the church. Read through Samuel J. Stone's hymn "The Church's One Foundation."

Chapter 12. And Finally

1. In preparation for this class session, it may be worthwhile to interview your pastor to determine your church's viewpoint on the end times.

2. Write the following questions on the board: "Do you think we are living in the last days? Why or why not?" After some responses have been given, ask the class what events are, according to Scripture, certain to happen in the future. Develop the discussion with selected material from the text.

3. Distribute to each class member a copy of your church's doctrinal statement. Note the section on the last things or the end times. How detailed is the sequence that is presented? On what biblical passages are these details based? How have other Christians interpreted these passages?

4. Proceed through the "Bible Investigation" in order to identify the chief purpose of prophecy. Enlarge on the discussion by using "For Further Thought" to discover some of the major themes of prophecy.

5. Present to the class the idea that an individual who understands the reasons why God has revealed what he has regarding the future should be motivated to believe in Jesus Christ. Use the "Personal Application" to point out the certainty of future judgment and the nature of true belief in Christ.

6. Note that discussions in Christian circles concerning future events all too often turn into very unchristian argumentative debates. It is important to remember that many strongly held convictions in this area will not be proven until God brings the present age to a close. A seventeenth-century Latin epigram will be helpful to keep in mind:

> In essentials, unity.
> In uncertainties, freedom.
> In all things, love.

Chapter 13. Epilog:
The Difference Belief Makes

1. Write the following questions on the board: "Are correct doctrinal beliefs essential to our having a satisfactory relationship with God? Why or why not?" Use the following Scripture

references to augment the discussion: Hebrews 11:6; Matthew 16:13–19; 1 John 4:2–3; Romans 10:9–10.

2. Review the evidences for the divine authorship of the Bible ("Key Question" 1). Include the Bible's own claims of divine origin (2 Sam. 23:2; Isa. 8:11; Jer. 30:4; Amos 3:1; Mic. 4:4; Acts 1:16; 3:18, 21; 4:25; 2 Tim. 3:16; 2 Pet. 1:20–21) as well as various external evidences—fulfilled prophecy, the continuity of the message, substantiation by historical research and archeology.

3. Divide the class into small groups of three or four in order to complete the "if . . . then" statements in "Key Question" 2. Share the results with the whole group.

4. Proceed through the "Bible Investigation" by assigning selected sections of Psalm 119 to small groups. Again, share the responses with the whole class.

5. Discuss the issues raised in "For Further Thought." You may wish to read Ephesians 4 and then ask the questions suggested in the "Personal Application."

6. Conclude with a reading of Psalm 1. Note the benefits which come to a person whose "delight is in the law of the LORD."